Steve Martin is one of today's most talented performers. He has had huge success as a film actor, with such credits as *Roxanne, Father of the Bride, Parenthood* and *The Spanish Prisoner*. He has won Emmys for his television writing and two Grammys for comedy albums. In addition to the bestselling *Pure Drivel*, he has written several plays, including *Picasso at the Lapin Agile*, and a highly acclaimed novel, *Shopgirl*. His latest novel, *The Pleasure of My Company*, is available in hardback from Weidenfeld & Nicolson. His work appears in *The New Yorker* and *The New York Times*.

D0682858

By Steve Martin

Pure Drivel
Picasso at the Lapin Agile
Shopgirl
The Pleasure of My Company

Pure Drivel

Steve Martin

PHOENIX

A PHOENIX PAPERBACK

First published in Great Britain in 1999
by Viking
First published in paperback with additional material in 2000
by Penguin Books
This paperback edition published in 2003
by Phoenix,
an imprint of Orion Books Ltd,
Orion House, 5 Upper St Martin's Lane,
London WC2H 9EA

First published in the USA in 1998
by Hyperion

A CIP catalogue record for this book
is available from the British Library.

ISBN 0 75381 395 5

Printed and bound in Great Britain by
Clays Ltd, St Ives plc

Contents

Acknowledgments

At the time of this writing, I have not worked in a movie for three years. During these years, in which I vowed to do nothing and leave myself alone about it, I accidentally produced several plays, a handful of sketches, two screenplays, and a reorganization of my entire self. The pieces in this book, these essays – I'm not sure what to call them – are little candy kisses, after-dinner mints to the big meal of literature, but to me they represent something very special. They are the offspring of an intense retrospection that enabled me to get back in contact with my work, to receive pleasure from my work, and to bring joy to my work. They also enabled me to repeat the phrase 'my work' three times in one sentence, which brought me a lot of joy, pleasure, and contact. I suppose what I'm saying is, if you really want to work, stop working.

I owe a big gooey blob of thanks to Chris Knutsen, who fearlessly and humorously edited the pieces that appeared in *The New Yorker*, and to Tina Brown, who charmed me and ran the pieces in a magazine I idolized for half my life, even when it gave me stinking movie reviews. And special thanks to Leigh Haber, who fastidiously edited each piece, both new and old, for this edition. Heavy mitting, also, to my agents Esther Newberg and Amanda Urban, who made sure Hyperion provided me with a full-time makeup artist and a trailer as big as Hemingway's during the writing of this book. Equal thanks, too, to my philosopher/lawyer Michael Gendler, who makes sure that my vulnerable artistic gentleness is always well paid.

I am lucky to have friends both literate and funny, and I'll cite Victoria Dailey, who first published my writing, in the days when the process of writing was so primitive the text was written by hand directly on the computer screen. Her personality and mind are such that she called me once at midnight and said, 'I figured out something about you. You're an *a* away from being a Martian.' She then cock-a-doodled a laugh and hung up.

I'd also like to mention good friends to whom I sent fledgling pages in hopes of getting back a critical or favorable comment. They are April Gornik, Jessica Teich, Kathy Goodman, and Elizabeth Meyer. I also have men friends.

A Public Apology

Looking out over the East River from my jail cell and still running for public office, I realize that I have taken several actions in my life for which I owe public apologies.

Once, I won a supermarket sweepstakes even though my brother's cousin was a box boy in that very store. I would like to apologize to Safeway Food, Inc., and its employees. I would like to apologize to my family, who have stood by me, and especially to my wife Karen. A wiser and more loyal spouse could not be found.

When I was twenty-one, I smoked marijuana every day for one year. I would like to apologize for the next fifteen years of anxiety attacks and drug-related phobias, including the feeling that when Ed Sullivan introduced Wayne and Shuster, he was actually signaling my parents that I was high. I would like to apologize to my wife Karen, who still believes in me, and to the Marijuana Growers

Association of Napa Valley and its affiliates for any embarrassment I may have caused them. I would also like to mention a little incident that took place in the Holiday Inn in Ypsilanti, Michigan, during that same time. I was lying in bed in room 342 and began counting ceiling tiles. Since the room was square, it was an easy computation, taking no longer than the weekend. As Sunday evening rolled around, I began to compute how many *imaginary* ceiling tiles it would take to cover the walls and floor of my room. When I checked out of the hotel, I flippantly told the clerk that it would take twelve hundred ninety-four imaginary ceiling tiles to fill the entire room.

Two weeks later, while attempting to break the record for consecutive listenings to 'American Pie,' I realized that I had included the *real tiles* in my calculation of imaginary tiles; I should have sub-tracted them from my total. I would like to apologize to the staff of the Holiday Inn for any inconvenience I may have caused, to the wonderful people at Universal Ceiling Tile, to my wife Karen, and to my two children, whose growth is stunted.

Several years ago, in California, I ate my first clam and said it tasted 'like a gonad dipped in motor oil.' I would like to apologize to Bob 'n' Betty's Clam Fiesta, and especially to Bob, who I found out later only had one testicle. I would like to apologize to the waitress June and her affiliates, and the DePaul family dog, who suffered the contents of my nauseated stomach.

There are several incidents of sexual harassment I would like to apologize for:

In 1992, I was interviewing one Ms. Anna Floyd for a secretarial position, when my pants accidentally fell down around my ankles as I was coincidentally saying, 'Ever seen one of these before?' Even though I was referring to my new Pocket Tape Memo Taker, I would like to apologize to Ms. Floyd for any grief this misunderstanding might have caused her. I would also like to apologize to the Pocket Tape people, to their affiliates, and to my family, who have stood by me. I would like to apologize also to International Hardwood Designs, whose floor my pants fell upon. I would especially like to apologize to my wife Karen, whose constant understanding fills me with humility.

Once, in Hawaii, I had sex with a hundred-and-two-year-old male turtle. It would be hard to argue that it was consensual. I would like to apologize to the turtle, his family, the Kahala Hilton Hotel, and the hundred or so diners at the Hilton's outdoor café. I would also like to apologize to my loyal wife Karen, who had to endure the subsequent news item in the

'Also Noted' section of the *Santa Barbara Women's Club Weekly*.

In 1987, I attended a bar mitzvah in Manhattan while wearing white gabardine pants, white patent-leather slippers, a blue blazer with gold buttons, and a yachting cap. I would like to apologize to the Jewish people, the State of Israel, my family, who have stood by me, and my wife Karen, who has endured my seventeen affairs and three out-of-wedlock children.

I would also like to apologize to the National Association for the Advancement of Colored People, for referring to its members as 'colored people.' My apology would not be complete if I didn't include my new wife, Nancy, who is of a pinkish tint, and our two children, who are white-colored.

Finally, I would like to apologize for spontaneously yelling the word 'savages!' after losing six thousand dollars on a roulette spin at the Choctaw Nation Casino and Sports Book. When I was growing up, the usage of this word in our household closely approximated the Hawaiian *aloha*, and my use of it in the casino was meant to express 'until we meet again.'

Now on with the campaign!

Writing Is Easy!

Writing is one of the most easy, pain-free, and happy ways to pass the time in all the arts. For example, right now I am sitting in my rose garden and typing on my new computer. Each rose represents a story, so I'm never at a loss for *what* to write. I just look deep into the heart of the rose and read its story and write it down through *typing*, which I enjoy anyway. I could be typing 'kjfiu joewmv jiw' and would enjoy it as much as typing words that actually make sense. I simply relish the movement of my fingers on the keys. Sometimes, it is true, agony visits the head of a writer. At these moments, I stop writing and relax with a coffee at my favorite restaurant, knowing that words can be changed, rethought, fiddled with, and, of course, ultimately denied. Painters don't have that luxury. If they go to a coffee shop, their paint dries into a hard mass.

I would recommend to writers that they live in California, because here they can look up at the blue sky in between those moments of looking into the heart of a rose. I feel sorry for writers – and there are some pretty famous ones – who live in places like South America and Czechoslovakia, where I imagine it gets pretty dreary. These writers are easy to spot. Their books are often depressing and filled with disease and negativity. If you're going to write about disease, I would suggest that California is the place to do it. Dwarfism is never funny, but look at the result when it was dealt with out here in California. Seven happy dwarfs. Can you imagine seven dwarfs in Czechoslovakia? You would get seven melancholic dwarfs at best, seven melancholic dwarfs with no handicapped-parking spaces.

Love in the Time of Cholera: *why it's a bad title*

I admit that 'Love in the time of . . .' is a great title, so far. You're reading along, you're happy, it's about love, I like the way the word *time* comes in there, something nice in the association of *love* and time, like a new word almost, *lovetime*: nice, nice feeling. Suddenly, the morbid *Cholera* appears. I was happy till then. 'Love in the Time of the Oozing Sores and Pustules' is probably an earlier, rejected title of this book, written in a rat-infested tree house on an old Smith-Corona. This writer, whoever he is, could have used a couple of weeks in Pacific Daylight Time.

I did a little experiment. I decided to take the following disheartening passage, which was no doubt written in some depressing place, and attempt to rewrite it under the influence of California:

Most people deceive themselves with a pair of faiths: they believe in *eternal memory* (of people, things, deeds, nations) and in *redressibility* (of deeds, mistakes, sins, wrongs). Both are false faiths. In reality the opposite is true: everything will be forgotten and nothing will be redressed. (Milan Kundera)

Sitting in my garden, as the bees glide from flower to flower, I let the above paragraph filter through my mind. The following new paragraph emerged:

I feel pretty,
Oh so pretty,
I feel pretty and witty and bright.

Kundera was just too wordy. Sometimes the delete key is your greatest friend.

Writer's Block: A Myth

Writer's block is a fancy term made up by whiners so they can have an excuse to drink alcohol. Sure a writer can get stuck for a while, but when that happens to real authors, they simply go out and get an 'as told to.' The alternative is to hire yourself out as an 'as heard from,' thus taking all the credit. It is also much easier to write when you have someone to 'bounce' with. This is someone to sit in a room with and exchange ideas. It is good if the last name of the person you choose to bounce with is Salinger. I know a certain early-twentieth-century French writer, whose initials were M. P., who could have used a good bounce person. If he had, his title might have been the more correct 'Remembering Past Things' instead of the clumsy one he used. The other trick I use when I have a momentary stoppage is virtually foolproof, and I'm happy to pass it along. Go to an already published novel and find a sentence you absolutely adore. Copy it down in your manuscript. Usually that sentence will lead you naturally to another sentence; pretty soon your own ideas will start to flow. If they don't, copy down the next sentence. You can safely use up to three sentences of someone else's work – unless they're friends; then you can use two. The odds of being found out are very slim, and even if you are, there's no jail time.

Creating Memorable Characters

Nothing will make your writing soar more than a memorable character. If there is a memorable character, the reader will keep going back to the book, picking it up, turning it over in his hands, hefting it, and tossing it into the air. Here is an example of the jazzy uplift that vivid characters can offer:

Some guys were standing around when in came this guy.

You are now on your way to creating a memorable character. You have set him up as being a guy, and with that come all the reader's ideas of what a guy is. Soon you will liven your character by using an adjective:

But this guy was no ordinary guy, he was a red guy.

This character, the red guy, has now popped into the reader's imagination. He is a full-blown person, with hopes and dreams, just like the reader. Especially if the reader is a red guy. Now you might want to give the character a trait. You can inform the reader of the character trait in one of two ways. First, simply say what that trait is – for example, 'but this red guy was different from most red guys, this red guy liked frappés.' The other is rooted in action – have the red guy walk up to a bar and order a frappé, as in:

'What'll you have, red guy?'
'I'll have a frappé.'

Once you have mastered these two concepts, vivid character writing combined with adjectives, you are on your way to becoming the next Shakespeare's brother. And don't forget to copyright any ideas you have that might be original. You don't want to be caught standing by helplessly while your familiar 'red guy' steps up to a bar in a frappé commercial.

Writing Dialogue

Many very fine writers are intimidated when they have to write the way people really talk. Actually it's quite easy. Simply lower your IQ by fifty and start typing!

Subject Matter

Because topics are in such short supply, I have provided a few for writers who may be suffering in the darker climes. File some of these away, and look through them during the suicidal winter months:

'Naked Belligerent Panties': This is a good sexy title with a lot of promise.

How about a diet book that suggests your free radicals *don't* enter ketosis unless your insulin levels have been carbo-charged?

Something about how waves at the beach just

keep coming and coming and how amazing it is (I smell a bestseller here).

'Visions of Melancholy from a Fast-Moving Train': Some foreign writer is right now rushing to his keyboard, ready to pound on it like Horowitz. However, this title is a phony string of words with no meaning and would send your poor book to the 'Artsy' section of Barnes and Noble, where – guess what – it would languish, be remaindered, and die.

A Word to Avoid

'Dagnabbit' will never get you anywhere with the Booker Prize people. Lose it.

Getting Published

I have two observations about publishers:

1. Nowadays, they can be either male or female.
2. They love to be referred to by the appropriate pronoun. If your publisher is male, refer to him as 'he.' If your publisher is female, 'she' is considered more correct. Once you have

established a rapport, 'Babe' is also acceptable for either sex.

Once you have determined your pronoun usage, you are ready to 'schmooze' your publisher. Let's say your favorite author is Dante. Call Dante's publisher and say you'd like to invite them both to lunch. If the assistant says something like 'But Dante's dead,' be sympathetic and say, 'Please accept my condolences.' Once at lunch, remember never to be moody. Publishers like up, happy writers, although it's impressive to suddenly sweep your arm slowly across the lunch table, dumping all the plates and food onto the floor, while shouting 'Sic Semper Tyrannis!'

A Demonstration of Actual Writing

It's easy to talk about writing and even easier to do it. Watch:

Call me Ishmael. It was cold, very cold, here in the mountain town of Kilimanjaroville.© I could hear a bell. It was tolling. I knew exactly for who it was tolling, too. It was tolling for me, Ishmael Twist,© a red guy who likes frappé. [Author's note: I am now stuck. I walk over to a rose and look into its heart.] That's right, Ishmael Twist.®

Finally, I can't overstress the importance of having a powerful closing sentence.

Yes, in My Own Backyard

Last week in Los Angeles, I realized that the birdbath in my garden is by Raphael. I had passed it a thousand times; so had many producers, actors, executives, and the occasional tagalong screenwriter. No one had ever mentioned the attribution 'Raphael.' In fact, none of my guests had bothered to attribute it at all, which surprised me since they spend so much time discussing it. When I try to steer the conversation around to my films, my television appearances, and my early work, all I hear back is: 'What a charming birdbath.' To me, this is further evidence that the birdbath is a Raphael: one just can't look away.

Much has been made of the fact that Raphael never sculpted. That may be true, but what is less known is that he designed many avian objects that we today take for granted, including the clothesline and the beak polisher. A birdbath is completely within the oeuvre of the master. Mine is stylistically characteristic of his work, including triangulation (inverted), psychologically loaded negative space, and a carved Madonna holding an infant who looks fifty. Identical birdbaths appear in thirteen of his paintings; there is a Vasari portrait of Raphael painting the birdbath, and there is a scribble in his last diary that in translation reads, 'Send my birdbath to Glendale,' which is where I bought it at a swap meet.

In every person there's an art expert, and I'm sure the one in you wants some proof of authenticity in this age where, every day, Rembrandt van Rijns are being demoted to Rembrandt Yeah Sures.

There are two ways of confirming a work of art: scholarship and intuition. As far as scholarship goes, you can imagine that my copy of *Raphael for Dummies* is now well thumbed in my quest for authentication. But I needed to find a latter-day Berenson to put the final nail in the coffin of confirmation. The Los Angeles phone book lists two Raphael scholars, although one has a Maui area code. Both have been called in, and they are unanimous in their conclusion: one for, one against. This kind of scholarship proves something, but it can never take you the last mile; it is intuition that confirms attribution every time. How many times have I sat in my garden with the cordless, sipping on a cocktail ice of Prozac and Halcion, ignoring the masterpiece that stood before me? However, everyone has experienced that moment when our inner censor slips away and the volume of our headnoise is turned down low and we realize we are sitting in front of Raphael's birdbath. It is a swooping cloak of *sureness*, which falls from heaven and settles over you.

At that moment, I decided there was only one way to finally confirm my intuition to the rest of the world. I would visit the tomb of Raphael, who is buried in the *Pantheon* in Rome, and commune with the great master himself. (I emphasize the Pantheon italically because, in my dyslexia, I read it as *Parthenon* and wasted money on a trip to Athens. I suggest a name change for one of them, to avoid confusion. After all, it's not like one is a river and one is an airport; they're both buildings.)

Entering the Pantheon, one cannot help but experience a feeling of awe. Looking to the left, one sees the hallowed name Pesto, to the right, a series of Popes and Pope wannabes. Unfortunately, they are not buried in alphabetical order, so finding Raphael was not easy. I skipped over him a couple of times, because evidently he had a last name and that threw me off. Forgive me, but if I'm looking for the grave of Liberace, I want it filed under Liberace, not Wladziu Valentino, etc. Madonna take note.

I stood before the vault where Raphael has lain for the last four hundred and fifty years. Before I relate to you the next part, I have to tell you a little bit about the Pantheon. It has the world's largest domed ceiling. A domed ceiling might be a big deal in the world of architecture, but in the world of whispering it is definitely lousy. Everything comes back to you three times as loud, and even your diction is cleaned up. So when I whispered, 'Did you make my birdbath?' everybody in the place heard me except Raphael, who was dead. I whispered again, louder, 'Did you make my birdbath?' A few minutes later, a man in a trench coat came up to me and said 'Yes, but the Wide Man wants a green lawn.' He then handed me an envelope containing five hundred million lire and slithered away.

The voice of Raphael did not come to me with his answer until several hours later, when I sat in a café within sight of the Pantheon, sipping a synthetic low-fat coffee mixed with a legal (in Italy) derivative of Xanax and Quaalude. The voice emanated directly from the Pantheon and headed across the square to where I was sitting. Raphael, who now must be in heaven and hence has access to practically everything, used Italian but subtitled it with a dialect only my sister and I spoke when we were five. It confirmed that the birdbath was his and that he wanted everyone to know he was not gay.

The Martin Birdbath, as some scholars are now calling it – I objected at first – is still in the garden, although attended by a twenty-four-hour armed guard named Charlie (he's off on the weekends), whom I have grown to like. I'm not quite sure he knows what he is guarding, but with the parade of academicians trooping through, he's got to figure that it ain't cheese. His job, in addition to keeping the birdbath from being stolen, is to keep birds away. This is hard, because to a bird, a birdbath is a birdbath, be it by Raphael or the Sears garden department.

Even though several offers have emerged, I'm not going to sell the Raphael. I'm not even going to mention it to my guests, unless I feel it's going to get me somewhere. I suppose if I see someone staring at it as though a boom has just been lowered on them, I'll take them aside and fill them in. I will tell them they are standing in the presence of a master, that they are in touch with the power of the ages, and that they deserve the overused but still meaningful hyphenation 'sensitive-type.' Then I will direct them to sit back in my Gauguin-designed lawn chair and enjoy the view. How do I know it's by Gauguin? It is. I just know it is.

Changes in the Memory after Fifty

Bored? Here's a way the over-fifty set can easily kill off a good half hour:

1. Place your car keys in your right hand.
2. With your left hand, call a friend and confirm a lunch or dinner date.
3. Hang up the phone.
4. Now look for your car keys.

(For answer, turn to page 24 and turn book upside down.)

The lapses of memory that occur after fifty are normal and in some ways beneficial. There are certain things it's better to forget, like the time Daddy once failed to praise you and now, forty years later, you have to count the tiles in the bathroom – first in multiples of three, then in multiples of five, and so on – until they come out even, or else you can't get out of the shower. The memory is selective, and sometimes it will select 1956 and 1963 and that's all. Such memory lapses don't necessarily indicate a more serious health problem. The rule is, if you think you have a pathological memory problem, you probably don't. In fact, the most serious indicator is when you're convinced you're fine and yet people sometimes ask you, 'Why are you here in your pajamas at the Kennedy Center Honors?'

Let's say you've just called your best friend, Joe, and invited him to an upcoming birthday party, and then, minutes later, you call him back and invite him to the same party again. This does not mean you are 'losing it' or 'not playing with a full deck' or 'not all there,' or that you're 'eating with the dirigibles' or 'shellacking the waxed egg' or 'looking inside your own mind and finding nothing there,' or any of the demeaning epithets that are said about people who are peeling an empty banana. It does, however, mean that perhaps Joe is no longer on the list of things you're going to remember. This is Joe's fault. He should have a more memorable name, such as *El Elegante*.

Sometimes it's fun to sit in your garden and try to remember your dog's name. Here's how: Simply watch the ears while calling out pet names at random. This is a great summer activity, especially in combination with Name That Wife and Who Am I? These games actually strengthen the memory and make it simpler to solve such complicated problems as 'Is this the sixth time I've urinated this hour or the seventh?' This, of course, is easily answered by tiny pencil marks applied during the day.

Note to self: Write article about waxy buildup.

If you have a doctor who is over fifty, it's wise to pay attention to his changing memory profile. There is nothing more disconcerting than patient and healer staring at each other across an examining table, wondering why they're there. Watch out for the stethoscope being placed on the forehead or the briefcase. Watch out for greetings such as 'Hello . . . you.' Be concerned if while looking for your file he keeps referring to you as 'one bad boy.' Men should be wary if, while examining your prostate, the doctor suddenly says, 'I'm sorry, but do I know you?'

There are several theories that explain memory problems of advancing age. One is that the brain is full: It simply has too much data to compute. Easy to understand if you realize that the name of your third grade teacher is still occupying space, not to mention the lyrics to 'Volare.' One solution for older men is to take all the superfluous data swirling around in the brain and download it into the newly large stomach, where there is plenty of room. This frees the brain to house relevant information, like the particularly troublesome days of the week. Another solution is to take regular doses of ginkgo biloba, an extract from a tree in Asia whose memory is so indelible that one day it will hunt down and kill all the humans that have been eating it. It is strongly advised that if taking ginkgo biloba, one should label the bottle 'Memory Pills.' There is nothing more embarrassing than looking at a bottle of ginkgo biloba and thinking it's a reliquary for a Spanish explorer.

So in summary, waxy buildup is a problem facing all of us. Only a good strong cleanser, used once or twice a month, will save us the humiliation of that petrified yellow crust on our furniture. Again, I recommend an alcohol-free, polymer-base cleanser, applied with a damp cloth. Good luck!

The car keys are in your hand. Please remember to turn the book right side up.

Mars Probe Finds Kittens

The recent probe to Mars has returned irrefutable evidence that the red planet is populated with approximately twenty-seven three-month-old kittens. These 'kittens' do not give birth and do not die but are forever locked in a state of eternal kittenhood. Of course, without further investigation, scientists are reluctant to call the chirpy little creatures kittens. 'Just because they look like kittens and act like kittens is no reason to assume they are kittens,' said one researcher. 'A football is a brown thing that bounces around on grass, but it would be wrong to call it a puppy.'

Scientists were at first skeptical that a kitten-type being could exist in the rare Martian atmosphere. As a test, Earth kittens were put in a chamber that simulated the Martian air. The diary of this experiment is fascinating:

6:00 A.M.: Kitten appears to sleep.

7:02 A.M.: Kitten wakes, darts from one end of cage to another for no apparent reason.

7:14 A.M.: Kitten runs up wall of cage, leaps onto other kitten for no apparent reason.

7:22 A.M.: Kitten lies on back and punches other kitten for no apparent reason.

7.30 A.M.: Kitten leaps, stops, darts left, stops abruptly, climbs wall, clings for two seconds, falls on head, darts right for no apparent reason.

7:51 A.M.: Kitten parses first sentence of lead editorial in daily newspaper, which is at the bottom of the chamber.

With the exception of parsing, all behavior is typical Earth-kitten behavior. The parsing activity, which was done with a small ballpoint pen, is considered an anomaly.

Modern kitten theory suggests several explanations for the kittens' existence on Mars. The first, put forward by Dr. Patricia Krieger of the Hey You Bub Institute, suggests that kittens occur both everywhere and nowhere simultaneously. In other words, we see evidence of kitten existence, but measuring their behavior is another matter. Just when the scientists point their instruments in a kitten's direction, it is gone, only to be found later in another place, perhaps at the top of drapes. Another theory, put forward by Dr. Charles Wexler and his uncle Ted, suggests that any universe where round things exist, from theoretical spheres to Ping-Pong balls, necessarily implies the existence of a Mover Kitten. The scientific world has responded by saying that the notion of the Mover Kitten is not a concern for legitimate research and should be relegated to the pseudoscientific world. The pseudoscientific world has responded by saying that at least three endorsements from independent crackpots are needed before anything can truly be called 'pseudo.'

Some have suggested that the hostility of the Martian climate should be enough to seriously set back the long-term prospects of any species. However, the weakness of Martian gravity is a bonus for felines. They are able to leap almost three times as high as they can on Earth. They can climb twice as far up a carpet-covered post, and a ball with a bell in it will roll almost three times as far. This is at least equal to the distance a mature poodle can roll a ball with its nose.

Even though there could be a big market on Earth for eternal kittens, most scientists agree that the human race should not pursue a further involvement.

There are those, however, who believe that having now discovered the creatures, we have a responsibility to 'amuse' them. Dr. Enos Mowbrey and his wife/cousin, Jane, both researchers at the Chicago Junebug Institute for Animal Studies, argue that the kittens could be properly amused by four miles of ball string cut into fourteen-inch segments. The cost of such a venture would be:

Four miles of string: $135
Segmentation of string: $8
Mars probe to deliver string and jiggle it: $6 trillion.

It is unfortunate that Dr. Mowbrey's work has been largely dismissed because of his inappropriate use of the demeaning term *kitty cat*.

The next time you look up at the heavens, know that mixed in the array of stars overhead is a pale-red dot called Mars, and on that planet are tiny creatures whose wee voices are about to be thunderously heard on this planet, a meow of intergalactic proportions.

Dear Amanda

Dear Amanda,

This will be the last letter I write to you. I think we have made the right decision. Thank you for your love. We had a wonderful experience these past five months. I want you to know that our time together will live inside me in a special place in my heart. It is best if we do not phone or write.

Love always,
Joey

Dear Amanda,

I dialed you last night because the *Lucy* pie episode was on and I knew you'd want to see it. Anyway, while I was leaving a message, I leaned on the phone and accidentally punched in your message-retrieval code. Sorry about that. Who's Francisco? Just curious.

Joey

Dear Amanda,

I realized that I still had your set of six Japanese sake cups that I bought for you on our trip downtown and was wondering when it might be a good time to drop them off. You can give me a call at the usual number but maybe better at the office up till seven but then try the car or I'm usually home now by seven forty-five. I would like to get these back to you, as I know you must be thinking about them. This will be my last letter.

Regards,
Joey

Dear Amanda,

It was a lucky coincidence that my cat leapt on your speed-dial button last night, as it gave us a chance to talk again. Afterwards, I was wondering what you meant when you said, 'It's over, Joey, get it into your head.' So many interpretations. Just curious. Oh, I found myself on your street last night and noticed a yellow Mustang that I don't remember ever being at your apartment complex. Is this the mysterious Francisco I've heard rumors about? No big deal. Just curious. I left one of the sake cups at your front door;

it happened to be in my car. What was that loud music?

> With respect,
> Joey

Dear Amanda,

This will be the last letter I write to you. I hate to hurt you like this, but I'm seeing someone new. You'd like her. Her name is Marisa – she has the same number of letters in her name as you! Incidentally, I heard that Francisco had or is having a tax problem. Should I meet with him? I'm over it all now and would be glad to help. Also, a word of warning: Latins. One woman is never enough. Just a thought.

> Joey

PS Do you have my red Pentel pen? I really need it. Page me when you get this.

Dear Amanda,

This will be the last letter I write to you. I'm quite upset that you changed your phone without a forwarding number. There could still be emergencies, and I'm still in possession of those fancy upholstered hangers of yours. Marisa questioned me about them the other day, and it wasn't fun. They're probably too dear to you to throw out, as we bought them together at the swap meet the day your mother raved about me, saying I was 'pleasant.' *Please* come by and pick them up; they're seriously damaging my relationship with Marisa. A good time would be any Wednesday after five but not after seven, Fridays anytime except lunch, Monday is good, and the weekend, anytime. Also Tuesday. By the way, there's someone named Francisco trying to pick up girls on the Internet. Hmm . . . I wonder.

Joey

Dear Amanda,

Valentine's Day is tomorrow, and I hope you don't mind my throwing this note through your window, as the post would be too slow. The rock it's tied to came from our desert trip! I'm wondering if you'd like to get together for a quick lunch on the fourteenth – you can even bring Francisco if you want; maybe I could help him sort out his heavy urology bills. I need to get my letters back from you, and could you bring this one too? I could bring the hangers, and I also want you to have the photo of me nude skydiving. Can you let me know soon? I'm waiting outside on the lawn.

This will be the last letter I write to you.

Love you always,
Joey

Times Roman Font Announces Shortage of Periods

Representatives of the popular Times Roman font, who recently announced a shortage of periods, have offered other substitutes – inverted commas, exclamation marks, and semi-colons until the period crisis is able to be overcome by people such as yourself, who, through creative management of surplus punctuation, can perhaps allay the constant demand for periods, whose heavy usage in the last ten years, not only in English but in virtually every language in the world, is creating a burden on writers everywhere, thus generating a litany of comments such as: What the hell am I supposed to do without my periods? How am I going to write? Isn't this a terrible disaster? Are they crazy? Won't this just create misuse of other, less interesting punctuation???

'Most vulnerable are writers who work in short, choppy sentences,' said a spokesperson, who added, 'we are trying to remedy the situation and have suggested alternatives like umlauts, as we have plenty of umlauts – in fact, more umlauts than we could possibly use in a lifetime; don't forget, umlauts can really spice up a page with their delicate symmetry, resting often midway in a word, letters spilling on either side, and can not only indicate the pronunciation of a word but also contribute to the writer's greater glory, because they're fancy, not to mention that they even look like periods, indeed are indistinguishable from periods, and will lead casual readers to believe the article actually contains periods!'

Bobby Brainard, a writer living in an isolated cabin in Montana, who is in fact the only writer living in an isolated cabin in Montana who is not insane, is facing a dilemma typical of writers across the nation: 'I have a sentence that has just got to be stopped; it's currently sixteen pages long and is edging out the front door and is now so lumbering I'm starting to worry that one period alone won't be enough and I will need at least two to finally kill it off and if that doesn't work, I've ordered an elephant gun from mail order and if I don't get some periods fast, I'm going to have to use it . . .' The magazine *International Hebrew* has issued this emergency statement: 'We currently have an oversupply of backward periods and will be happy to send some to Mister Brainard or anyone else facing a crisis!'

.period backward the in slip you while moment a for way other the look to sentence the getting is trick only The

The concern of writers is summed up in this brief telegram:

Period shortage mustn't continue stop
Stop-stoppage must come to full stop stop
We must resolve it and stop stop-stoppage stop

Yours truly,
Tom Stoppard

Needless to say, there has been an increasing pressure on the ellipsis . . .

'I assure you,' said the spokesperson, 'I assure you the ellipsis *is not* – repeat, is *not* – just three periods strung together, and although certain writers have plundered the ellipsis for its dots, these are deeply inelegant and ineffective when used to stop a sentence! ¿An ellipsis point is too weak to stop a modern sentence, which would require at least *two* ellipsis periods, leaving the third dot to stand alone pointlessly, no pun intended, and indeed two periods at the end of a sentence would look like a typo . . . comprende? And why is Times Roman so important? Why can't writers employ some of our other, lesser-used fonts, like Goofy Deluxe, Namby-Pamby Extra Narrow, or Gone Fishin'?' In fact, there is movement toward alternate punctuation; consider the New Punctuation and Suicide Cult in southern Texas, whose credo is 'Why not try some new and different types of punctuation and then kill ourselves?' Notice how these knotty epigrams from Shakespeare are easily unraveled:

Every cloud engenders not a storm ☺
Horatio, I am dead ☹

Remembering the Albertus Extra Bold asterisk embargo of several years back, one hopes the crisis is solved quickly, because a life of exclamation marks, no matter how superficially exciting, is no life at all! There are, of course, many other fonts one can use if the crisis continues, but frankly, what would you rather be faced with, Namby Pamby Extra Narrow or the bosomy sexuality of Times Roman? The shortage itself may be a useful one, provided it's over quickly, for it has made at least this author appreciate and value his one spare period, and it is with great respect that I use it now.

Schrödinger's Cat

A cat is placed in a box, together with a radioactive atom. If the atom decays, a hammer kills the cat; if the atom doesn't decay, the cat lives. As the atom is considered to be in either state before the observer opens the box, the cat must thus be considered to be simultaneously dead and alive.

ERWIN SCHRÖDINGER'S CAT PARADOX, 1935

Wittgenstein's Banana

A banana is flying first class from New York to L. A. Two scientists, one in each city, are talking on the phone about the banana. Because it is moving in relationship to its noun, the referent of the word *banana* never occupies one space, and anything that does not occupy one space does not exist. Therefore, a banana will arrive at JFK with no limousine into the city, even though the reservation was confirmed in L. A.

Elvis's Charcoal Briquette

A barbecue is cooking wieners in an airtight space. As the charcoal consumes the oxygen, the integrity of the briquette is weakened. An observer riding a roller coaster will become hungry for wieners but will be thrown from the car when he stands up and cries, 'Elvis, get me a hot dog.'

Chef Boyardee's Bungee Cord

A bungee cord is hooked at one end to a neutrino, while the other end is hooked to a vibraphone. The neutrino is then accelerated to the speed of light, while the vibraphone is dropped off the Oakland Bay Bridge. The cord will stretch to infinite thinness, the neutrino will decay, and the vibraphone will be smashed by the recoiling bungee. Yet an observer standing on the shore will believe he hears Tchaikovsky's second piano concerto performed by Chef Boyardee's uncle Nemo.

Sacajawea's Rain Bonnet

Lewis and Clark are admiring Sacajawea's rain bonnet. Lewis, after six months in the wilderness, wants to wear the rain bonnet, even when it's not raining. Clark wants Sacajawea to keep wearing it and doesn't want to have to deal with Lewis, who conceivably could put on the bonnet and start prancing. However, an observer looking back from the twenty-first century will find this completely normal.

Apollo's Non-Apple Non-Strudel

Imagine Apollo running backward around the rings of Saturn while holding a hot dish of apple strudel. In another universe, connected only by a wormhole, is a dollop of vanilla ice cream. The vanilla ice cream will move inexorably toward the wormhole and be dumped onto the strudel. Yet wife swapping is still frowned upon in many countries.

Jim Dandy's Bucket of Goo

Jim Dandy is placed in a three-dimensional maze. His pants are tied at the ankles and filled with sand. Every time he moves to another dimension of the maze, he must review the movie *Titanic*, first with one star, then with two stars, then with three, while never mentioning its box office take. If he completes the maze, he will then be able to untie his pant-legs, and the spilling sand will form a bowling trophy that Jim Dandy may take home.

The Feynman Dilemma

A diner says to a waiter, 'What's this fly doing in my soup?' And the waiter says, 'It looks like the backstroke.' Yet if the same scene is viewed while plunging into a black hole at the speed of light, it will look like a Mickey Mouse lunch pail from the thirties, except that Mickey's head has been replaced by a Lincoln penny.

George Hamilton's Sun Lamp

George Hamilton is dropped into an empty rental space next to a tanning salon on the dark side of the moon. There is no way into the salon except through an exterior door, but if George exits, it could mean dangerous exposure to deadly gamma rays. George could open his own tanning salon by tapping the phone lines from next door and taking their customers. And yet George is cooked when he exits the rental space while using a silver-foil face reflector.

Taping My Friends

Jerome

(friend, 22 years)

ME: . . . Does your wife know?

JEROME: I hope she doesn't find out.

ME: Find out what?

JEROME: What I told you yesterday.

ME: Right. I remember what you told me yesterday, but the way you said it was so poignant. Would you say it?

JEROME: I just don't want her to find out about my having a drink with that waitress. I was so dumb.

ME: So you definitely had a drink with the waitress.

JEROME: [*Inaudible*]

ME: Sorry?

JEROME: Yes.

ME: Yes, what?

JEROME: I had a drink with the waitress.

ME: Whose name was?

JEROME: Dinah. Are you having memory problems?

ME: Yes. Could you recap?

JEROME: I had a drink with the waitress, Dinah.

ME: Let's keep this between us.

JEROME: Thanks, man.

Virginia

(ex-girlfriend)

VIRGINIA: I'm feeling so guilty about what we did.

ME: Can you hang on a minute?

[Sound of beep from tape recorder being turned on]

VIRGINIA: What was that?

ME: What?

VIRGINIA: That beep.

ME: Federal Express truck backing up. You feel guilty about what?

VIRGINIA: You know, the other night. I'd feel terrible if Bob ever found out.

ME: How would he ever find out?

VIRGINIA: So you won't tell?

ME: I can't believe you're asking me that.

VIRGINIA: I'm sorry.

ME: Find out about what?

VIRGINIA: You know. The kiss and the . . . you know.

ME: It was beautiful. I'd love for you to describe it.

VIRGINIA: What a nice thing; you're so romantic now. When we were dating, I couldn't believe how cold you were, and how selfish . . .

[*Sound of tape recorder being turned off*]

[*Pause*]

[*Sound of tape recorder being turned back on*]

VIRGINIA: . . . ask for separate checks, you big loser. What was that beep?

ME: FedEx truck again, but get back to the kiss.

VIRGINIA: Well, we had just had lunch and you walked me back to my apartment and we kissed by the mailboxes, and you know.

ME: Who is we again?

VIRGINIA: We? You and I.

ME: And your name is?

VIRGINIA: Are you insane? I'm Virginia!

ME: I love it when you say your name . . .

Wilhelmina

(business acquaintance)

ME: It's nice walking along the lake, isn't it, Wilhelmina?

WILHELMINA: Oh, yes, it's very nice. That sure is a nice flower on your lapel . . .

[Snifffff]

ME: Wilhelmina, I was wondering if you ever see, say, my ex-wife's new husband's tax return when you're working over there at the IRS?

WILHELMINA: Oh yes, I do, but I would never –

[Thud thud thud thud]

ME: I'm sorry, what was that?

WILHELMINA: I was saying that I would never reveal –

[Thud thud thud thud]

ME: Wilhelmina, please don't poke me on the lapel like that.

WILHELMINA: Sorry . . .

Mom

(mother)

ME: Mom, I'm really in a hurry, and I can't remember what you told me twelve years ago about how upset you were with Dad's false tax return.

MOM: Well, let me think. I think he had under-reported some income on his night job . . . we were so desperate. Remember you needed that extra money for college?

ME: Oh yeah.

MOM: You needed money for . . . I can't remember.

ME: To buy SAT answers.

MOM: I can't hear you, son.

ME: I said – what was that beep?

MOM: FedEx truck backing up. You were saying?

ME: I needed cash to buy answers for my college entrance exam. But that's between us, Mom.

MOM: Of course, son. If you can't trust your mother, who can you trust?

The Nature of Matter and Its Antecedents

I was taking a meeting with my publicists last week, trying to figure out what to do next. Marty suggested that the audience wants a Steve Martin to be doing a comedy right now. Tony said that a Steve Martin should do a nice cameo in a drama, 'kind of an award thing.' Michelle's idea was different, 'Jack has a Légion d'honneur; let's get you a Nobel. Why not make a profound scientific discovery and then write an essay about it? This is what the public wants right now from a Steve Martin.' I had never thought of myself as a Steve Martin before, but I guess I was one, and frankly, it felt good.

'Go on,' I implored.

'Well, maybe you could write something on matter, or the nature of matter. Cruise is doing something on reverse DNA. You could do something too. Maybe better.'

'The problem is it's not matter I'm interested in. It's prematter. The moment when it's "not soup yet," when it's neither nothing nor something.'

'Steve, isn't that really just semantics?' said Michelle. 'You're talking about something existing prior to existing.' I looked at her and thought how stupid she was.

'Now you're talkin' like Bruce and Demi,' I said. 'Did you see their piece in *Actor/Scientist*? I would love to attack their semantics angle.'

Michelle inched forward. 'Why don't you, Steve?' I realized she had maneuvered me into acceptance.

I remembered when Stallone had turned in his first *Rambo* draft. Through all the rewrites, he was also quietly conducting experiments on the irregular movements of explosive sound. He conjectured that explosive sound will travel faster through air already jarred by another explosion, with the bizarre effect that between two simultaneous explosions, a perceiver will hear the farther explosion first. The studio head told me later that the studio wasn't too confident in the script at the time, but the scientific work was so fascinating, they decided to let Stallone keep writing. Sly asked for no public acknowledgment of his work but diligently spent hours editing to make sure the movie's sound corresponded to reality.

The next day I had my noon shrink appointment, and luckily we got into Spago at a corner table. I talked openly about my fears of winning a Nobel, and I also admitted my concerns about getting airline reservations and decent hotel rooms in Stockholm during prize season. My shrink reminded me that there were personal rewards for writing a scientific essay: the satisfaction of doing something for no other reason than to do it well. My other shrink disagreed. I have a call into my third, 'tiebreaker' shrink.

That night I was in a limo with Sharon Stone having sex and stopped for a minute with the question 'Can something be in a state of becoming but not yet exist?' Sharon crossed her legs as only she can and said something so profound that everything in me tingled. 'In Swahili it can. Now, where were we?' In her words was my answer to Bruce and Demi: *Only in English and other Germanic derivatives must a thing exist prior to its existence.* Sharon's publicist leaned forward. 'Go on, Sharon, I'm very curious about what you're meaning.' Sharon explained further: 'After all, you're not talking about a grape becoming a raisin; you're talking about the interstitial state between pure nothing and pure something.' I looked down. I was still tumescent. Then she added, 'Who made your sunglasses?' 'They're Armanis. I saw them at his store in Boston, but they were on sale, so I waited and got them at Barney's at full price.'

We finally arrived at The Ivy, where we were to meet Travolta, Goldie and Kurt, Tom and Nicole, and Sly for dinner. Our table wasn't ready, so we yanked some tourists off their table and took their food.

We talked through the evening. Sly astounded us by coming up with nine anagrams of the word *Rambo*, Travolta amused the table by turning our flat bottle of Evian into gassy Perrier by simply adding saltpeter and rubber shavings. Kurt and Goldie discussed their cataloging of 'every damn grasshopper in Colorado.' Tom mentioned that he could cure the common cold in four seconds with a vacuum gun, except for the pesky weakness of the eardrums, which tended to dangle outside the ears after treatment. Our publicists stood behind us as we ate, and one of them wisely noted that it renews the soul to do something for yourself, something that you don't market in Asia, and we all acknowledged the truth of that. Of course, every time the waiter or a fan would approach the table, we quickly turned the topic of conversation to Prada leather pants, because for that night, anyway, we decided to keep our little secrets.

I drifted off for a few moments and thought about my paper. As much as I wanted to be known for my science writing and for it to be published under my own name, I also knew it might cost me the Nobel if I did. The committee would probably be disinclined to give an award to any man who has worn a dress to get a laugh from a monkey. I thought about publishing the essay under a pseudonym, like Stiv Morton or Steeve Maartin, in order to deceive the Nobel committee. My reverie was broken by Nicole, who asked the table, 'Why do we do it, this science?' No one had an answer, until I stood up and said, 'Isn't there money in a Nobel?'

The Sledgehammer: How It Works

Many of today's adults, who are otherwise capable of handling sophisticated modern devices, are united by a contemporary malady: sledgehammer anxiety. 'I feel I'm going to break it'; 'The old ways still work for me'; 'This is where technology leaves me behind,' are the most common chants of the sledgehammerphobe. Much of this initial fear comes from a failure to understand just how it works. By attaching a 'heavy weighted slug' to a truncated super-cissoid, a disproportionate fulcrum is created. In other words, if you're a TV set showing Regis promoting a diet book, and you're in a room with an angry unpublished poet holding a sledgehammer, watch out.

The novice sledgehammerer (from the German *sledgehammeramalamadingdong*) must be familiar with a few terms:

Thunk: the sound the 'clanker' (street term for 'heavy
   weighted slug') makes when wielded against the
   'stuff' (see next)
Stuff: things that are to be wanged (see next)
Wang: the impact of the clanker and the stuff
Smithereens: the result of being wanged

Many people are surprised to find out that the
sledgehammer has only one moving part: it. Yet
'Should I buy now or wait for the new models?' is a
refrain often heard from the panicky first-timer, who
forgets that the number of sledgehammer innovations
in the last three thousand years can be counted on one
finger. There are currently only two types of sledgehammer on the market: the three-foot stick with
a lead weight on the end, called the 'normal,' and a
new model, currently being beta-tested, which is a
three-foot stick with a lead weight in the middle,
called the 'below normal.' But don't let market confusion keep you from getting your feet wet. The
longer you wait, the fewer things you will demolish.

'There is a natural fear of sledgehammers,' says the
National Sledgehammer and Broken Toe Society,
which, in response, has been charting the most
common accidents and offers tips for the sledgehammer's safe use. The over-the-head position, for

example, often leads to excruciating lower body pain, caused when the sledgehammer wedges itself between the thighs at the end of the backswing. There is also the self-inflicted back-of-the-head knockout on lateral swings, which is very rare, and only afflicts – to use the researcher's lingo – 'really dumb people.' There are also cleaning accidents. A home hobbyist in Valdosta, Georgia, reported that while he was removing paint from his sledgehammer, it suddenly went out of control and destroyed his living room wall, even though he never let go of its handle.

Despite all these drawbacks, the world of the sledgehammer is rife with enthusiasts. 'I find the sledgehammer very erotic,' says Jane Parpadello, who is a stockbroker with Smith Barney and wants everyone to know her home phone number is listed. 'I think it's because my father was shaped like a sledgehammer: the long wooden body and big metal head. Today when I see a man with that shape, I want to pick him up and swing him against an apartment wall.'

The sledgehammer king, Marty Delafangio, whose net worth has been estimated at forty-two thousand dollars, was recently summoned before Congress to defend his reasons for attaching a mandatory Web-browser to his market-leading product.

'I smelled money to be made,' said Delafangio. 'The combination of a Web-browser and a sledgehammer is a natural.' Congress disagreed, and now the Web-browser can be sold only as an option, although, as a compromise, the powder-puff attachment remains.

Roustabouts have also noted a sharp increase in sledgehammer interest. 'We used to raise a circus tent pretty much on our own,' says Toby, a twenty-four-year veteran of Barnum & Bailey. 'Now I have crazies every morning from the local sledgehammer club, watching me plug a spike; it's a disgusting, circuslike atmosphere. One of them interviewed me for his newsletter. I let him take a swing too. He looked like Tinker Bell trying to lift a semi by its hood ornament. But it's not all bad; at least there's a never-ending supply of chicks. Although once some woman picked me up by the ankles and slammed me against an apartment wall.'

In the last ten years, the sledgehammer has come into its own, finally recognized for what it is: a tool, a thing, and a heavy object. Hundreds of years from now, when technology has altered the sledge-hammer's appearance into a sleek, digital, aero-dynamic *über*machine, it will no doubt function as it does today, toppling the mighty and denting the hard.

The Paparazzi of Plato

TABLOIDUS: Socrates, I wanted to show you my new Nikon fm2 with its six-hundred-millimeter lens.

SOCRATES: Thank you. It looks fine for taking pictures of ducks flying off in the distance.

MO-PED: That is a very fine purpose in combination with a speed bike and infrared night scope.

CLOOLUS: What else do you photograph, besides nature studies?

TABLOIDUS: I love to photograph children.

SOCRATES: That is a good and noble profession.

TABLOIDUS: There is nothing more beautiful to photograph than a mother breast-feeding her baby. Especially if it's Madonna.

CLOOLUS: You photographed Madonna breast-feeding her baby?

TABLOIDUS: Oh yes.

SOCRATES: What was she like in person?

TABLOIDUS: Well, I actually didn't meet her.

SOCRATES: Was she so full of herself that she wouldn't speak to you?

TABLOIDUS: Oh no. Because of the lens, I had to be three hundred yards away and shoot through her bedroom window.

CLOOLUS: It seems odd to me that Madonna would agree to have herself photographed this way.

TABLOIDUS: Her agreement was tacit.

CLOOLUS: But it seems to me you have invaded her privacy.

SOCRATES: Cloolus, what is privacy?

CLOOLUS: Privacy is the state of being secluded from the view of others.

SOCRATES: Are you private when you are alone in a crowded market?

CLOOLUS: Certainly not.

SOCRATES: Are you private when you're alone in a car?

CLOOLUS: More so, Socrates.

SOCRATES: Are you private when you're in a car with tinted windows?

CLOOLUS: That is starting to be private.

SOCRATES: Are you private when you're in your home?

CLOOLUS: Certainly.

SOCRATES: Is it not true that if you tint your

windows or stay home, in some way you are protecting your privacy?

MO-PED: It cannot be otherwise.

CLOOLUS: But Madonna was in her home.

SOCRATES: Yes, but her windows were not tinted with UV 40 Reflecto-coat, nor was she alone.

MO-PED: She was with her baby!

SOCRATES: Therefore, she was not protecting her privacy, and how can one invade what is not protected?

CLOOLUS: I am confused.

SOCRATES: Can something be tinted and not tinted at the same time?

CLOOLUS: It would be impossible.

SOCRATES: Can something be private and public at the same time?

CLOOLUS: They are mutually exclusive.

SOCRATES: And is it not true that privacy and UV 40 Reflecto-coat are one and the same?

MO-PED: He has proved it!

SOCRATES: Tabloidus, where were you when you took the picture?

TABLOIDUS: I was hiding on a rooftop. Further, I was wearing black clothing and a hood.

SOCRATES: So you were merely protecting your privacy, while Madonna invaded your camera lens?

TABLOIDUS: I cannot argue otherwise, Socrates.

CLOOLUS: But is it not wrong to spy on a woman breast-feeding her baby?

MO-PED: When you become a singing star, it is wrong to want your breast-feeding to be private.

CLOOLUS: But why?

TABLOIDUS: Because of the public's right to know.

SOCRATES: Is it not true, Cloolus, when the public is shopping in a supermarket, very often at the checkout point, it has an overwhelming desire to see Alec Baldwin's newborn or Frank Gifford having sex?

CLOOLUS: I cannot deny it.

SOCRATES: This desire, known in a democracy as 'the checkout point of freedom,' is important, because without it, Frank's children would never have known about his transgression.

CLOOLUS: Your argument is flawless. But why was there never a similar desire to see, say, Jimmy Stewart having sex?

SOCRATES: Because Jimmy Stewart didn't have 'that special something.'

TABLOIDUS: Alas, Cloolus, the public's taste in those days was not so sophisticated.

CLOOLUS: So I am living in a wonderful age.

MO-PED: There could not be one finer!

SOCRATES: Let us now try and get a snapshot of Plato and Aristotle cavorting on a nude beach. It might pay for lunch.

Side Effects

Dosage: Take two tablets every six hours for joint pain.

Side Effects: This drug may cause joint pain, nausea, headache, or shortness of breath. You may also experience muscle aches, rapid heartbeat, or ringing in the ears. If you feel faint, call your doctor. Do not consume alcohol while taking this pill; likewise, avoid red meat, shellfish, and vegetables. Okay foods: flounder. Under no circumstances eat yak. Men can expect painful urination while sitting, especially if the penis is caught between the toilet seat and the bowl. Projectile vomiting is common in 30 percent of users – sorry: 50 percent. If you undergo disorienting nausea accompanied by migraine with audible raspy breathing, double the dosage. Leg cramps are to be expected; up to one knee-buckler per day is allowable. Bowel movements may become frequent, in fact every ten minutes. If bowel movements become greater than twelve per hour, consult your doctor, or in fact any doctor, or anyone who will speak to you. You may find yourself becoming lost or vague; this would be a good time to write a screenplay. Do not pilot a plane, unless you are in the 10 percent of users who experience 'spontaneous test pilot knowledge.' If your hair begins to smell like burning tires, move away from any buildings or populated areas and apply tincture of iodine to the head until you no longer hear what could be considered a 'countdown.' May cause stigmata in Mexicans. Do not sit on pointy conical objects. If a fungus starts to grow between your eyebrows, call the *Guinness Book of Records*. Do not operate heavy machinery, especially if you feel qualified for a desk job; that's good advice anytime. May cause famine and pustules. There may be a tendency to compulsively repeat the phrase 'no can do.' This drug may cause visions of the Virgin Mary to appear in treetops. If this happens, open a souvenir shop. There may be an overwhelming impulse to shout out during a Catholic mass, 'I'm gonna wop you wid da ugly stick!' You may feel a powerful sense of impending doom; this is because you are about to die. Men may experience impotence, but only during intercourse. Otherwise, a powerful erection will accompany your daily 'walking around time.' Do not take this product if you are uneasy with lockjaw. Do not be near a ringing telephone that works at 900 MHz, or you will be very dead, very fast. We are assuming you have had chicken pox. You also may experience a growing dissatisfaction with life, along with a deep sense of melancholy – join the club! Do not be concerned if you arouse a few ticks from a Geiger counter. You might want to get a one-month trial subscription to *Extreme Fidgeting*. The hook shape of the pill will often cause it to get caught on the larynx. To remove, jam a finger down your throat, while a friend holds your nose to prevent the pill from lodging in a nasal passage. Then throw yourself stomach-first on the back portion of a chair. The expulsion of air should eject the pill out of the mouth, unless it goes into a sinus cavity or the brain. WARNING: This drug may shorten your intestines by twenty-one feet. Has been known to cause birth defects in the user retroactively. Passing in front of a TV may cause the screen to moiré. While taking this drug, you might want to wear something lucky. Women often feel a loss of libido, including a two-octave lowering of the voice, an increase in ankle hair, and perhaps the lowering of a testicle. If this happens, women should write a detailed description of their last three sexual encounters and mail it to me, Bob, trailer 6, Fancyland Trailer Park, Encino, CA. Or e-mail me at 'hotguy.com.' Discontinue use immediately if you feel your teeth are receiving radio broadcasts. You may experience 'lumpy back' syndrome, but we are actively seeking a cure. Bloated fingertips on the heart-side hand are common. Be sure to allow plenty of 'quiet time' in order to retrain the eye to move off stationary objects. Flotation devices at sea will become pointless, as the user of this drug will develop a stone-like body density; therefore, if thrown overboard, contact your doctor. This product may contain one or more of the following: bungee cord, plankton, rubber, crack cocaine, pork bladders, aromatic oils, gum arabic – pardon me, an Arab's gums – gunpowder, corn husk, glue, bee pollen, English muffins, poached eggs, ham, hollandaise sauce, and crushed saxophone reeds. Sensations of levitation are illusory, as is the feeling of a 'phantom third arm.' User may experience certain inversions of language: Acceptable: 'Hi, are how you?' Unacceptable: 'The rain in Sprain slays blainly on the phsssst.' Twenty minutes after taking the pills, you will experience an insatiable craving to take another dose. AVOID THIS WITH ALL YOUR POWER. It is advisable to have a friend handcuff

65

you to a large kitchen appliance, ESPECIALLY ONE
THAT WILL NOT FIT THROUGH THE DOORWAY
TO WHERE THE PILLS ARE. You should also be
out of reach of any weaponlike utensil with which
you could threaten friends or family, who should
also be briefed to not give you the pills, no matter
how much you sweet-talk them. *Notice*: This drug
is legal in the United States only when the user is
straddling a state line.

Artist Lost to Zoloft

Performance artist Shelf Head 3 has decided to cancel his work 'Frog Slave' and instead open a creperie in Brooklyn so he can live closer to his parents.

'This change is not related to my recent prescription for the mood-elevating drug Zoloft,' said Shelf Head 3, who now prefers to be called Jeremy. 'I find I can say things with a crepe that I just couldn't say through urine writing. The first day on the job, I created – and I say created because that's exactly what I did – a *croissant distant*, loosely translated as a "faraway pie." Because that's what we are, really, aren't we? At night, after dinner with the folks, I would listen to Yanni, but I stopped because, well, he's so *angry*.

'I'm also changing my mural in Bilbao. Murals don't really have to cover an entire wall. It's obtrusive to the weekend driver. Why not a picket-fence-high depiction that the eye can *choose* to see rather than be forced to see? Maybe with tips for the marooned motorist on how to change a tire; perhaps with line three having a satirical swipe at the current administration. I'd like that. *Touché!* In fact, why not an info-mural? A product tie-in would make a point.

'My early works "Parent Kill" and "Why not me, Mom?" have been criticized as "juvenile, wasteful, boring, and why leave out disgusting?" Which was exactly the point, and subsequently, "juvenile, wasteful, boring, and why leave out disgusting?" became the name of our movement. Let me remind you that at one time *impressionism* and *fauve* were derogatory terms. However, my new work, which I will do on Sundays, when the creperie is closed, makes the same point in a stronger way: I'm going to darn a hundred pair of socks while watching *The Brady Bunch*. The point is self-explanatory, which is part of its meaning. Obscurity used to turn me on, but I'm either through with that phase or high. I also won't be doing my performance piece "Ear Slice" anymore – I've done it once, and I would like to retain my remaining lobe, as I'm finding it useful for hearing orders at the creperie.'

A Worrying Effect

The use of Zoloft in the artistic community has a worrying effect on art dealers selling to the 'anger market.' 'I can sell antiparent symbolist stuff all day,' said an unidentified dealer, 'but the artists aren't delivering it anymore. One artist, who used to give me birth canals with fangs, now sends me paintings of dogs playing poker. Who am I going to sell that to? English decorators who need fifty puppy pictures for a theme in the den, and that's all. The artist says his point is that although dogs playing poker has been painted many times before, it's usually bulldogs playing draw poker; there's still much to explore in lowball and stud. He also wonders why there's never been a wiener dog in these paintings. I just stare at him. I hate to think what would have happened to Jackson Pollock when the Zoloft kicked in. We may have to divide downtown galleries into zones, so that the collectors on Prozac can easily find the galleries on Prozac, and the ones on Zoloft don't accidentally wander into a Valium gallery. I used to worry about these issues, until I started on Zoloft myself so I could understand just what exactly my artists were painting.

'I have actually resorted to breaking into my artists' medicine cabinets and substituting their Zoloft with placebos, just enough for a week or two,' continued the dealer. 'This sudden withdrawal sends them on a wild emotional ride. Then I call Ernie's Artistic Supplies and have them deliver canvas, paints, and palette knives while the artists are still bouncing off the walls. Two weeks later, I get half a dozen canvases that are at least salable. Then the artists get back on the real pills, not knowing what hit them, and I start getting the Lassie-at-the-card-club stuff. I ship them off to Asia and tell the artists they were sold, crossing my fingers that they never go shopping at the Thailand airport mall.'

The artist Screaming Mimi, now Kathy, has summed up this problem nicely in her recent work 'I Enjoy Being a Girl.' The work consists of a lovely moonscape, with an accompanying explanatory note that hangs beside it. It should be noted that the effect of the Zoloft was wearing off as the painter reached midsentence:

I hope you all enjoy this painting, where the moon symbolizes the light of mystery, the misty damp air recalls the fog of ignorance, and the sea below it represents my desire to put you on a plate and eat you with a power tool.

How I Joined Mensa

I started with the phone book. Looking up Mensa was not going to be easy, what with having to follow the strict alphabetizing rules that are so common nowadays. I prefer a softer, more *fuzzy* alphabetizing scheme, one that allows the mind to float free and 'happen' upon the word. There is pride in that. The dictionary is a perfect example of overalphabetization, with its harsh rules and every little word neatly in place. It almost makes me want to go on a diet of grapes and waste away to nothing.

Being a member of Mensa means that you are a genius, with an IQ of at least 132. This enables you to meet other members, who will understand what the hell you are talking about when you say, for example, 'That lamppost is tawdry.' That's the kind of person they're after. Joining Mensa instills in you a courtly benevolence toward nonmembers who would pretend to know what you know, think what you think, and stultify what you perambulate.

I worried that the 132 cutoff point might be arbitrary until I met someone with an IQ of 131, and honestly, he was a bit slow on the uptake. If you have a dinner party of 132s and there's a 131 attending, you can actually feel the 131er hit the wall of stupidity. He acquires that dog look – the one with the wide eyes and the cocked head and the big grin – which tells you he's just not getting it. But unlike a dog, your guest cannot be put out in the yard to play with a ball, unless it has been agreed on beforehand.

I gave up on the phone book, which led me astray time and again with its complex passages, and then tried blind calling, with no success. Next, 1–800- MENSA, which weirdly brought dead silence on the other end of the phone. A week later, while *volksvalking*, I realized that MENSA didn't contain enough numerals to be a phone number and knew it must be some kind of test: any future member should be able to figure out the next two digits in the sequence. I tried dialing MENSANE, MENSAIL, MENSAFE, and MENSAPS, but I got three rebuffs and a fax tone.

So it was a complete accident that I stumbled into a party in my building, having inverted my floor number and gotten off at 21 instead of 12. Slipping past the first bloc of chatterers and avoiding the host, whom I identified through deduction, I flipped back the Oushak rug and counted the knots per square inch. These people had money. I heard snippets of conversation; words like *feldspar* and *eponym* filled the air. In the corner, a lone piper played a dirge. I knew where I was. This was a Mensa party.

That's when I saw Lola. She had hair the color of rust and a body the shape of a Doric column, the earlier ones, preinvasion. She walked across the room carrying one of those rum drinks and endearingly poked herself in the face with her straw as she slid herself onto the blue velveteen sofa. If she truly was Mensa, she would have no problem with my introduction. 'Please don't relegate me to a faraway lea,' I ventured.

'I can see you've read Goethe, the Snooky Lanson translations,' she countered. 'Lozenge?'

I was pegging her around 140. Her look told me she had put me in the low 120s. My goal was to elevate her assessment and wangle a Mensa membership form out of her. Taking a hint from soap operas, I talked to her with my back turned while staring out a window. 'Wouldn't you rather parse than do anything?' I queried. 'Hail Xiaoping, the Chinese goddess of song,' she rejoined.

Lola then engaged in some verbal sparring that left me reeling. 'This is quite an impressive apartment,' she offered.

I saw a dictionary on its stand. Oh, how I longed to run to it and look up *impressive*! How I wanted to retort in Mensa-ese! I felt the dog look creeping over my face, but it was my turn, and I spoke: 'I'm not sure if that's a compliment or an insult.' I threw my head back, laughing, coughed out my lozenge, and watched it nestle into the Oushak. She asked me my name. 'Call me Dor.' Later, I realized I meant 'Rod.'

Lola and I sat and talked through the night. After the party, I held her and whispered, 'I love that you're in Mensa.' She whispered back, 'I love that you're in Mensa too.' My temperature dropped to arctic. She told me her phone number, but since it was all sevens, I couldn't remember it. Then she walked to the elevator, turned back toward me, and said, 'We have to stop meeting like this.' Those words hit me like tiny arrows in the heart. That night, I cried and cried into my pillow. Eight months later, it was explained to me that it had been a joke.

Most things one wants in life come when they are no longer needed. My membership was awarded exactly one year later, when I applied and became an honorary Mensa 'plaything.' Answering a brochure ad that came with my introductory packet, I went on a Mensa love boat trip to Bermuda. Embarking, I saw a woman standing aft, her back to me, bent slightly over the railing, looking very much the way a Doric column would look if it were bent over a railing. She turned and saw me, and I again saw my Lola. It was as though nothing had changed in a year, because we were both wearing the same thing we wore on that first night, still unwashed. She spoke: 'Long time no see, Dor.'

I corrected her, gaining the upper hand: 'My name's not Dor.'

'What is it?' she asked.

'It will come to me.'

'Would you like to take a walk on the boat deck?' she asked.

Boat deck? Where is the damn dictionary when you need it?

She spoke: 'I have only two years to live. Let's enjoy them while we slaver.'

'Then slaver we shall, slaver we shall.' I took her hand and we turned eastward, toward the setting sun. 'And by the way, I think my name is Rod.'

Michael Jackson's Old Face

The things I could have said!

I would have loved being at a dinner party years from now, cocking an eyebrow at an old friend, while an invited guest whispered some choice gossip. I would have loved sending a silent message about someone I work with, by glancing down, a quiet smile breaking at the corners of my mouth, or by a tiny disapproving shake of the head. As my talent shifts in strength from year to year, I would have loved showing a wise acceptance of my successes and failures, with nothing more than a simple look. I would have liked entering a room and acknowledging an acquaintance with a nod, or snubbing an enemy, or withering a bitter critic with my indifference.

Luckily, I am able to have lunch once a week, at Jones' Grill on Melrose, with Walter Matthau's face and imagine how things might have been. Walter orders paradoxically, and his eyes shine as he looks over to include me in the joke. He then brings a smile to his face, which creeps irresistibly onto the waiter's face, and the waiter then shuffles his feet and returns to Walter a sly look of respect. I order coldly, free of nuance. I have a salad.

Walter's face understands my problem, so he doesn't demand much. I tell my tales in the midwestern style, sometimes choosing the right words, sometimes not finding them, but always unable to fill them in, to color them, to give them the triple-layered meaning or send them to him with a shimmer and a spin. But Walter's face doesn't mind; he accents the words for me, reacts for me, illustrating the expressions that are just out of my reach.

After a drink, Walter's face reminisces; his eyes fill, and a potential tear decides whether to let go. Finally, the weight of the water pulls it down the craggy slopes, where it dissolves and finally disappears into a hundred rivulets. My own sympathetic tear never hesitates; it speeds down along the Teflon and lands on nothing except the hard Formica tabletop. But Walter knows what I mean.

Later, I walk to the car, where my people wait, unable to interpret my mood, offering me things I don't want, not reading in my face that I would like to be alone.

That night, I lie behind my new face, speaking to it. It listens, but it can't say much back. Sometimes I feel a muscle twitching in response, reaching back toward me, trying to speak. I listen carefully, as Walter would, to expressionless lips whispering, 'What will I tell my child? How, when I am dying and unable to speak, will I look into his eyes and say I love you?'

In my dream that night, I see the image of serenity crossing my face, softening the mask. I sit and drink tea. My old face looks out the window and sees Walter, who signals approval with a fleshy smile. I stand; my pain moves up from the heart and into my face and dissipates. Then the happiness comes; next, the grief; then the joy. They all come up from the center, leaving traces of themselves in my brow, the corners of my mouth and eyes, my lips – and so revealing my character. I wake, momentarily feeling whole, but then I remember: The face reveals the heart, but sometimes it's easier to change the face.

In Search of the Wily Filipino

We have seen the slit-eyed dangerous Jap, we have seen the wily Filipino . . .

MARLON BRANDO, discussing movies on
Larry King Live

The wily Filipino. How often have I gone to bed at night with that phrase echoing through my head. And yet only recently I became aware that I had never actually seen one. I had driven through Filipino neighborhoods, but everyone and everything I saw was rather straightforward. Signs signifying this or that — the dry cleaner, the auto repair — all seemed innocuous, but probably hid a true guile lurking underneath. I wondered under what circumstance the wiliness would come out. I have worked with a Filipino for several years, and I decided to try a little test. I asked her what she would do if she saw a traffic accident and someone were wandering around looking dazed. 'I would stop and help, I suppose,' she said. 'Why?' I asked. 'To get something?' She looked at me and retorted, 'What would you do – call for help and wait for someone to show up?' I realized she was invoking the stereotype of the Benign and Polite WASP. I was so upset that it almost made me want to be angry.

I decided to rent movies in which I might examine the portrayal of the Filipino. I looked at *The Godfather, 2001*, and *Gone With the Wind*. There was not one depiction of a Wily Filipino. Why? Perhaps the movie industry is secretly run by Filipinos. Perhaps it was they who had been the hidden hand behind such films as *The Logical Filipino* (1986), *The Straight-up Guy from Manila* (1993), and the adventure film *Deep in Wily Laos* (1995). And if that was true, wouldn't it demonstrate unquestionable guile?

A friend of mine told me about a sensational Filipino acupuncturist, and I called to make an appointment. 'What seems to be the problem?' a deceptively pleasant voice asked on the other end of the line. 'I . . . I . . .' I hadn't quite worked out this part of the plan. I hung up. Thirty seconds later, the phone rang. There was no one there. I thought nothing of it, then soon recognized the craft and mechanics at work: Caller ID! The wily Filipino had called me back with caller ID and now had my number! Fearing reprisal, I redialed and booked an appointment.

I entered the office and sat in the waiting lounge. 'Waiting for what?' I wondered. Probably waiting to be out-foxed, one way or another. The assistant asked me to fill out a form. She cleverly slid the sheet toward me and artfully offered me a pen. As I filled out the form, I listened to the coded dialogue that went on in the office. Common inquiries about the weather were no longer empty pleasantries; they were complexly structured sentences in which the first letters of every word combined to spell out my mother's maiden name. Once in the office, I started using words with the doctor and his nurse that were uniquely American. Words like *cahoots*. I wanted to see their reaction. I got none – well, one, a look so wily I shuddered.

Then this exchange happened:

'It says here you want treatment for parvo.'

'Yes.' I countered. This game was rough.

'Parvo is a dog disease.'

The lake of perspiration on my forehead instantly beaded into a map of Michigan.

'Yes,' I replied. 'I'm worried that my dog may have it.'

'So you're here for anxiety? You want me to treat you for worry?'

This was not just idle sparring between two worthy foes. This was a coded chess play of words, a dazzling display of cunning.

The needles went in. Four in my ears. Three in my scalp. Some were twisted by hand; some had electric current sent through them. Ten minutes later, they were removed, and I felt remarkably calm. *The tables had been turned*. The wily, crafty Filipino had allayed my anxiety, and now I was indebted to him. He had won. I had anticipated some form of wiles, but I never suspected it would be at this level of sophistication.

I returned home and the *Larry King Show* was still on:

'. . . the luckless Italian, the furtive Chilean, the horny Hawaiian, the pungent Norwegian, the strict Eskimo, the loud-talking Canadian . . .'

'We're running out of time,' said Larry, and the show came to a close.

I needed to get away. I packed my bags, booked a ticket on WILY (the official Filipino airline), and flew to Hawaii.

Bad Dog

'You're a bad dog, a very bad dog!' shouts Dr. Fogel.

I'll show you what a bad dog is, thinks Jasper, padding down the hallway to his dog bowl, where he can think.

Sulking next to his dish, Jasper tries to sort everything out. The FedEx man is supposed to be barked at, dammit. When he is outside the gate, he is outside the threshold of recognition. As he nears, he comes inside the threshold of recognition. Of course I'm going to bark at him, even if I know who he is. The plumber is even lower than the FedEx man. I'm just saying, Watch out, he's got a wrench. Is that so terrible?

The cat slinks by. Jasper thinks the one epithet he could never say: Fraidy.

In the next room, Dr. Fogel is on the phone. 'Well, I need that package today, doggone it.' Jasper shudders. I hate it when he uses that word. Does he know how it hurts me? Does he know what he's saying? Why can't he say Goddammit, like everyone else? Goddammit is a decent, benign swear word, no matter how you look at it. Even backward, it's . . . it's . . . oh my dog!

The doorbell rings. Jasper's up and running to the front door, barking. Master and dog arrive at the same time. 'Quiet, Jasper! Quiet!' says Dr. Fogel, but Jasper can't keep quiet. The door opens. It's the FedEx man.

Oops, thinks Jasper. He immediately puts his nose between the deliveryman's legs. They love this; this will be my salvation, he calculates.

But from above he hears, 'Bad dog! Bad, bad dog.'

What? Bad dog? Jasper keeps on the happy face but is killed inside. He watches the exchange of signature and receipt, then follows Him, hoping for a pat or a word of understanding or just anything. It does not come.

Jasper dips into his bowl of water, hiding his big sad eyes. This is a major, major problem, he thinks. That night, lying on his sawdust-filled bed, Jasper realizes that there's something in his brain telling him to distinguish between the Federal Express man, who must be barked at in all circumstances, and Granny Fogel, for whom he demonstrates his admiration by rolling over and showing his genitals. But how can I stop myself from doing what I want to do — nay, what I must do? This urge is so strong, based on so many factors, so many subtle discernments. He decides that he lacks some key piece of information, some general rule of understanding that would put him on the clear path. He resolves to search for that knowledge by taking a trip around the world. For Jasper, the world is defined by a five-foot fence that surrounds his yard, the house, and all its contents.

The next morning, Jasper is out early. He sidles along the fence, hugging the wall, nose lowered into the grass. After an hour, he realizes that what he's doing is pointless, except for the pure fun of it all. He hangs around the kitchen for a while, doing the big-eyes thing, but gets nothing. Unrewarded, he moves to his bed for a snooze. Jasper puts his nose next to his last saved biscuit and nuzzles it. He thinks, Questing is hard, and he rolls over on his back, sticks his legs in the air, and falls asleep.

Falling hard into a dream, Jasper imagines himself paddling through the air in a vast gallery of paintings. Although he's never actually been to a museum, he once guided himself accidentally through London's Tate Gallery Internet site (the letters T - A - T - E are all left-handers on a keyboard, and one lucky paw slap sent Jasper spiraling into cyberspace). Now, in his dream, he is able to whirl and twist in the air, viewing the pictures up close and reading their museum labels. His dream, swirling up from his simple unconscious, changes each painter's bio: 'Johann Fuseli, Swiss painter and former dog.' 'Giovanni Battista Tiepolo, Italian painter and former dog.' Jasper sees that these artists have transformed the canine within themselves into wonderful works of art.

The doorbell jars Jasper out of his sleep. Consciousness takes over, and the beautiful dream fades back into his thin cortex. Rising, he looks through a series of windows, from the bedroom to the kitchen, and beyond the kitchen to the street. He sees the white rectangle of the FedEx truck. Impulsively, he runs toward the front door.

Charging down the hall, he can feel the bark welling up inside him. He is like a boxer with a coiled left hook about to be thrown, like the clapper of an alarm, already in motion toward its bell. He knows what he is facing: the cold censure of his master, balanced by the deliciously frightened face of the FedEx man. The bark churns deep within him. He feels it in his belly, moving up through his lungs. His body chemistry pumps him forward like a jockey's whip, and he turns the corner to the foyer.

There in gleaming white is the target, handing over the trim FedEx box to Jasper's beloved and vulnerable master. As he slows, the fleshy part of his paws struggling against the hardwood floor, Jasper's locomotion compresses his energy, forcing the bark into his throat. With his master looking on, he opens his mouth; the bark now lies just behind his tongue. As it rolls over the damp, spongy, pink surface, the miracle that is Art rises from his shallow unconscious and transforms the sound waves, curving the pointy spikes of the highs and rounding the crevices of the jagged lows. Jasper looks up at his master, and out comes, in a lovely baritone:

We're having a heat wave
A tropical heat wave . . .

Now there is not a sound. A performer's eon passes: the time between the final note of the aria and the whooshing, enveloping applause of the audience. Finally, into the silent ethereal mist that swarms in Jasper's head, comes his master's voice: 'Good boy – you're a good, good boy.'

Jasper turns, feeling the euphoric relief of an adrenaline shutdown. He moves away from the door. The cat walks by. There but for the grace of God go I, thinks Jasper. He walks into the kitchen, laps some water, looks back at the startled tableau by the front door, and goes outside to lie in the sun.

Hissy Fit

Let us assume there is a place in the universe that is so remote, so driven by inconceivable forces, where space and time are so warped and turned back upon themselves, that two plus two no longer equals four. If a mathematician were suddenly transported and dropped into this unthinkable place, it is very likely that he would throw a hissy fit. This is exactly what happens when a New York Writer contemplates, talks about, or, worst of all, is forced to visit Los Angeles.

It must be understood that the New York Writer is not necessarily a writer from New York. At home on the East Coast somewhere – it could even be Rhode Island – he is an individual, unique in every respect, defiantly singular and stylistically distinct. But when the assignment comes in, by fax or phone, to fly to Los Angeles and interview a poor-sap movie producer (poor sap because his ego leads him to believe that he will be the first of his kind to come off well), the proud author's metamorphosis begins. As the specter of California rises like a werewolf's moon, the mantle of New York Writer descends from the heavens and lands on his epaulets.

The ticket arrives by messenger and is subjected to much investigating and cross-checking to verify that it is truly round trip. Confusing words like *temblor* and *Knott's Berry Farm* drift in and out of his consciousness, and he wonders about the special mores of a thong-based culture.

The incidence of the hissy fit has risen in direct proportion to the airlines' cutbacks in oxygen levels on New York-Los Angeles flights. The longer flight time from east to west convinces our sojourner that even the headwinds are telling him not to go. It deprives his brain chemistry of valuable happiness molecules and gives him an agonizing arrival headache. He reads the *Los Angeles Times* on the plane and is disturbed by the typeface. Then, landing in the bright California sun after leaving New York on a cold, sunless day, he becomes doubly irked when he realizes he has left his sunglasses behind. Walking down the concourse, he sheds his forty-pound overcoat, peeling down to his wool shirt and furry vest. Now, overheated and overloaded, he recalls the words of a wheezing and sniffling SoHo gallery owner: 'I was just in LA and got a raging cold in that ninety-degree heat,' not recognizing in this unscientific pronouncement that if Los Angeles were an ethnic group, the comment would be a slur. Thus the hissy fit begins: The open palms move reflexively to the ears, in a nice approximation of Munch's *The Scream*. Nervous brain impulses tap out in Morse code, 'I am not one of you . . . I don't belong here . . . are there any others like me I can talk to?' Oddly, these thoughts are from the same writer who has climbed gun towers in Bosnia and gone undercover in street gangs.

Furthering the agony, the beleaguered writer finds himself in a rental car on the San Diego freeway and realizes he does not remember how to drive.

After pulling into the Mondrian Hotel on Sunset and striking a concrete pylon and maybe the valet parker, the writer slips and slides across the glassy floor of the lobby to the reception desk. To his left, he can see past the maître d's podium and the Armani-model hostess to an outdoor restaurant, crowded with people dressed in vinyl and other sauna-inducing unwearables. Behind him, the Beautiful Ones pose themselves around a sofa, and a tiny voice in his head whispers, 'You will never have them, because you have not been professionally groomed.'

The hissy fit is sustained throughout the day by an unpleasant cranial crowding of facts, comments, and sights, all of which must be simultaneously remembered, until the writer can unsheathe his computer and download his brain. Invited to the producer's house that evening for cocktails, the writer sees in the backyard of the subject's minivilla a gravity-defying bronze sculpture of a teen-on-a-swing, and a fiberglass rock over which a man-made waterfall flows. The writer now must chant over and over to himself, 'Remember the fiberglass rock.' Eventually, the producer greets him and clasps his hand, capturing his audience. One sentence later, he intimately reveals that his therapy involves talking to a doll of himself. Now the writer, with hours to go before ten-thirty, when the party will sputter and die, must keep repeating to himself, 'Remember the fiberglass rock, remember he talks to a doll . . . fiberglass rock, talks to doll, teen-on-a swing.' This keeps him from taking a deep breath and from noticing that the spreading sunset has saturated the air with a soft orange glow, almost like Paris, and that the view to the ocean is dappled with cottages nestled in a hillside, their lights just flickering on, almost like Portofino. He fails to see that Los Angeles is a city of abundant and compelling almosts.

The journey from the producer's house to the Mondrian Hotel, through an accordion descent of roads from the hills to the flats, requires the navigational skills of Magellan. Driving under the sky with one star, he is still intoxicated by the dizzying combination of white wine, party dresses, and a sense of not belonging, while a truth unfolding outside his windshield goes unobserved: The New York grid of streets and avenues, with its intellectual sectors leading to artistic quarters leading to shopping Edens, does not lie correctly over this Los Angeles sprawl. For the Los Angeles grid is warped, like the assumed mathematical netherworld, and must be moved through in an illogical manner. As the surface is unpeeled, a deeper level is revealed, but just below that the surface level appears again. This effect leaves the writer seeing only quark smoke trails, the evidence of something richer that has been missed.

At last, he is back in his hotel room, which unfortunately faces east into the now dead-black hills. Had his room been facing west, he would have noted the sparkling twenty-five-mile vista to the sea, which looks almost like the Mediterranean. He would have noted how the streets of LA undulate over short hills, as though a finger is poking the landscape from underneath. How, laid over this crosshatch, are streets meandering on the diagonal, creating a multitude of ways to get from one place to another by traveling along the hypotenuse. These are the avenues of the tryst, which enable Acting Student A to travel the eighteen miles across town to Acting Student B's garage apartment in nine minutes flat after a hot-blooded phone call at midnight. Had he been facing seaward on a balcony overlooking the city, the writer might have heard, drifting out of a tiny apartment window, the optimistic voice of a shower singer, imbued with the conviction that this is a place where it is possible to be happy. He would have seen, above the rolling rows of houses, the five or six aircraft that are always floating motionlessly over the city, planes that now so directly connect to his jet lag, which is mysteriously working in reverse: Even though it's 3:00 A.M. in the east, he is wide awake. Instead, he observes how the hilltops have been shorn into mesas to accommodate someone's Palladian-Tudor-Gothic-French-fantasy *palais*, and as it's too late to call a sympathetic ear in New York, he heads to the lobby bar.

The bar is alive, and he falls into a conversation with Candy. Candy is either nineteen or twenty-five or thirty-two, and she pronounces her belief in the powers of the amethyst around her neck as fervently as Constantine for the Church of Rome. The writer knows that next week this belief will be forgotten, or replaced by another, and he remembers it for his article. The hissy fit prevents him from seeing that Candy carries around an even sillier and more poignant belief, one that must be maintained and renewed daily: that she is in possession of a talent that will lift her to the stars. This belief permeates LA's soil; it is in the cars, in the clothes, and in the conversations of the up-and-coming. It is a far-fetched religion, which works often enough to sustain a supply of new believers, and it becomes the mantra of every hopeful, regardless of education or class. The writer looks at the explosion of hair sitting opposite him and puts her in a convenient niche, missing the point that the foolish can't write, but boy, can they act.

After a limp and sexless blackout sleep at the hotel, the writer, with a hangover and no sunglasses, waits for his prey at a staggeringly sunny outdoor café.

The producer, after having called the restaurant twice, each time warning of a fifteen-minute delay, sweeps in a half hour late but with an on-time feeling and cuddles fully half the diners before sitting down. So now two stereotypes, one that is lived daily and the other acquired for the journey, sit opposite each other. The writer needs no tape recorder, since it is not the words that will be reported but only the facts, observable and imagined, that fit the thesis. The hissy fit settles in nicely and filters everything through its eyes. Forty minutes later, the cell phone that is lying on the table vibrates across it, and the meeting is over.

Returning to an already dark New York City on the welcoming shorter flight home, the writer arrives at the melodious and historic acronym JFK and not the atonal, punning LAX. The hissy fit begins to subside. Soothed by the familiar jolts of a taxi ride and a one-hour view of the Beloved City from the gridlocked Triborough Bridge, the writer arrives home with a laptop full of judgments. The autopsy is faxed in, gleefully edited and published, then distributed proudly to concurring family and friends. The New York Writer lies back on his bed, adjacent to the clanging radiator where a rented copy of the producer's latest flop has accidentally melted into a horseshoe. He falls asleep, under the sky with no stars, his grasp slowly loosening from his manuscript, never dreaming that one should not ridicule one's foolish, fun, poetic cousin.

Drivel

Dolly defended me at a party. She was an artist who showed at the Whitney Biennial, so she had a certain outlook, a certain point of view, a certain under-standing of things. She came into my life as a stranger who spoke up when I was being attacked by some cocktail types for being the publisher of *American Drivel Review*. It wasn't drivel that I published, she explained to them, but rather the *idea* of drivel.

One drink later, we paired off. She slouched back on the sofa with her legs ajar, her skirt draped between them. I poured out my heart to this person I had known barely ten minutes: how it was hard to find good drivel, even harder to write it. She knew that to succeed, one must pore over every word, replacing it five or six times, and labor over every pause and comma.

I made love to her that night. The snap of the condom going on echoed through the apartment like Lawrence of Arabia's spear sticking in an Arab shield. I whispered passages from *Agamemnon's Armor*, a five-inch-thick romance novel with three authors. She liked that.

As publisher of *ADR*, I never had actually written the stuff myself. But that morning, arising with a vigor that had no doubt spilled over from the night before, I sat down and tossed off a few lines and nervously showed them to Dolly. She took them into another room, and I sat alone for several painful minutes. She came back and looked at me. 'This is not just drivel,' she exulted. 'It's *pure* drivel.' The butterflies in my stomach sopranoed a chorus of 'Hallelujah.'

That night, we celebrated with a champagne dinner for two, and I told her that her skin was the color of fine white typing paper held in the sun and reflecting the pink of a New Mexican adobe horse barn.

The next two months were heaven. I no longer just published drivel; I was now writing it. Dolly, too, had a burst of creativity, which sent her into a splendid spiraling depression. She had painted a tabletop still life that was a conceptual work in that it had no concept. Thus the viewer became a 'viewer,' who looked at a painting, which became a 'painting.' The 'viewer' then left the museum to 'discuss' the experience with 'others.' Dolly could take the infinitesimal pause to imply the quotations around a word (she could also indicate italics with just a twist of her voice).

Not wanting to judge my own work or to trust Dolly's love-skewed opinion, I sent my pieces around and made sure they were rejected by five different magazines before I would let myself publish them in *Drivel Review*. Meanwhile, fueled by her depression, Dolly kept producing one artwork after another and selling them to a rock musician with the unusual name of Fiber Behind, but it kept us in doughnuts and he seemed to really appreciate her work.

But our love was extinguished quickly, as though someone had thrown water from a high tower onto a burning dog.

What happened was this: Dolly came home at her usual time. What I had to tell her was difficult to say, but it somehow came out with the right amount of effortlessness, in spite of my nerves.

'I went downtown and saw your new painting of a toaster at Dia. I enjoyed it.'

She acknowledged the compliment, started to leave the room, and, as I expected, stopped short.

'You mean you "enjoyed" it, don't you?' Her voice indicated the quotation marks.

I reiterated, 'No, I actually enjoyed it.'

Dolly's attention focused, and she came over and sat beside me. 'Rod, do you mean you didn't go into the "gallery" and "see" my "painting"?' I nodded sadly.

'You mean you saw my painting without any irony whatsoever?' Again, I nodded yes.

'But, Rod, if you view my painting of a toaster without irony, it's just a painting of a toaster.'

I responded, 'All I can tell you is that I enjoyed it. I really liked the way the toaster looked.'

We struggled through the rest of the night, pretending that everything was the same, but by morning it was over between us, and Dolly left with a small 'goodbye,' soaking with the irony I had come to love so much.

I wanted to run, run after her into the night, even though it was day, for my pain was bursting out of me, like a sock filled with one too many bocce balls.

Those were my final words in the last issue of *Drivel Review*. Since then, I have heard that Dolly spent some time with Fiber Behind, but I'm sure she picked up a farewell copy and read my final, short, painful burst of drivel. I like to think that a tear marked her cheek, like the trace of a snail creeping across white china.

I Love Loosely

RICKY: Lucy, I'm home!

LUCY: Oh, hi, Ricky. How were things at the club today?

RICKY: Oh, fine.

LUCY: What did you do?

RICKY: The usual – rehearsed a new number and had sex with an usherette.

LUCY: *Waaaaaaaa!*

RICKY: Lucy, what's the matter?

LUCY: You said you had sex with an usherette . . . *Waaaaaaaa!*

RICKY: Lucy, don't be silly. It was only oral sex.

LUCY: It was?

RICKY: Of course, Lucy.

LUCY: It wasn't intercourse?

RICKY: Of course not, Lucy. That would be cheating.

LUCY: Oh, Ricky, I almost forgot those passages from the Bible you read to me that proved it.

RICKY: Now I'm goin' to change, and you go make dinner.

LUCY: Yes, Ricky.

(*Ricky exits. Lucy goes to the phone.*)

LUCY: (*On the phone*) Ethel?

ETHEL: (*On the phone*) What is it this time, Lucy?

LUCY: Ethel, I'm not so sure about this 'oral sex is not cheating' business.

ETHEL: This is not another one of your schemes, is it?

LUCY: Oh no, Ethel. It's just that Ricky claims it says so in the Bible.

ETHEL: Well, Lucy, why don't you ask a monsignor?

LUCY: Where would I find one?

ETHEL: There's one in the building. Mrs. Trumble has one visiting her now. You want me to send him down?

LUCY: Thanks, Ethel.

(*There is a knock at the door. Lucy answers. It's the monsignor.*)

LUCY: That was fast!

MONSIGNOR: Hello, Mrs. Ricardo. It says right here in Leviticus that oral sex is not cheating.

LUCY: How did you know what I wanted to ask?

MONSIGNOR: It's the only thing people have been asking me for months. Men have been joining

our church by the thousands! Ah . . . ah . . . *ah
choo*!

(*The monsignor's mustache flies off.*)

LUCY: *Fred*!

FRED: Lucy, this was all Ricky's idea!

(*Ricky enters.*)

RICKY: Lucy, is my dinner ready? (*He sees Fred and
starts swearing in Spanish.*)

(*Ethel enters, sees the mustache on the floor, picks it
up, and hands it to Fred.*)

ETHEL: Here, put this on your bald head for old
times' sake.

LUCY: But how did Ricky know I was worried that
oral sex was actually cheating?

ETHEL: I've been taping all your phone conversations and selling them to him, Lucy.

LUCY: But, Ethel, you're my best friend!

ETHEL: I was getting even with you for making me
wear that cat suit to the Beverly Hills Hotel.

RICKY: Ethel, tell Lucy you're sorry.

ETHEL: Oh, all right. Lucy, I'm sorry I taped all
your phone calls and ruined your life.

LUCY: And Ricky, I'm sorry I thought you had
intercourse when it was just oral sex.

(*They all hug.*)

FRED: Can I take off my wire now, Ricky?

Lolita at Fifty

Lolita Haze, now Guccioni (though currently single), angled her shopping cart and knelt down for the bottle of fallen fabric softener that her sashaying walk had knocked into the aisle. 'Let me get that,' mooned a stock boy, and Lolita, peering over her sunglasses, breathed, 'I've got it.'

The usual crowd had gathered at one end of the aisle, knowing that Lolita herself would be doing the retrieval, but it was the rear view from the checkout stand that was the best: the accordion bend of the long body, the knees locked but the ankles splayed, her arms becoming longer than her entire folded frame as she reached, and the slight shift to translucence of the yellow mini as it stretched in response to the breathtaking bend. A shudder traveled up the hierarchy of the supermarket, from box boy to general manager. Even the security camera ground to a halt in the middle of its traverse.

Rolling her way to the checkout stand, a teenage

cashier only recently elevated from box boy quickly hid the Ten Items or Less sign, hoping to encourage Lolita to come his way. Paying with a check at a snail's pace, she delicately wrote her signature with a heart-dotted *i*, an action that had three purposes: the first was to sign the check, the second was the three-quarters lean-over that caused a jittery eye motion from the box boy, and the third was to raise the back of her short blouse inches above the yellow mini, creating a three-hundred-and-sixty-degree sphere of influence.

Once in the parking lot, Lolita propped herself against her yellow Miata, idly tapping the heel of her half-dislodged shoe against the asphalt, using her toe as a motor. A sweating thirteen-year-old loaded her bags into the trunk. She broke her akimbo slouch (Lolita was rarely not akimbo; in fact, her third husband, Mark, observed that at any given moment, a randomly selected part of her body was always catty-corner to another) and drifted over to the remaining plastic bag full of apples, in a manner so lazy that even after the walk was over, it seemed as though it hadn't happened. She hoisted the bag lazily in a locked fist and rested it against the back of her raised forearm, slung the bag into the trunk with a slew-footed twist, and handed the gaping boy a single. Reading his name tag, she raised her eyes and gave him a 'Thank you, Rory.'

The boy replied, 'Thank you, Miss . . . Miss . . .'

'Lo-lee-tah,' she tongued. A column of sweat drained down the boy, and he entered puberty.

As she made the twenty-minute drive down Ventura Boulevard in the endless California sun, Lolita's mind grew active. 'I'm tired of ranch style,' she thought as she pulled into the driveway of the house she had lived in through the tenure of two husbands. Inside, she struck her thinking pose, notching her hip against the kitchen counter and hanging one arm on a cabinet pull. 'I'm forty-five years old,' she lied to herself. 'Perhaps it's time for a change.' She thought a nice apartment on the LA side of the Hollywood Hills, where there were more people like her, would do her fine.

Lolita had never had a snap of trouble selling any of her houses. She had a real estate license, and as long as one of the prospective buyers was male, all she had to do was be there while the couple poked through the house. Men felt a powerful drive to be in a room with her, especially after seeing her boudoir, which rivaled a house of mirrors. On the vanity stood an array of lipsticks stacked like ammo, which, incidentally, is exactly what they were. A sliding door revealed a closet filled with a rainbow of stretch pants, infinitely reflected from wall to wall. Lolita's skills were such that the wives always remained oblivious to their husbands' deepening interest in velour. She would follow the prospective buyers into the kitchen, where she would lounge indolently in a doorway and point things out by waggling a banana. The husbands would then jump to buy the house, just so they might be in the same room with her at the closing.

This time, however, while waiting for the buyer's inevitable yes, Lolita was experiencing a nagging pull at her psyche: she felt a desire to work. This was a monumental shift in her thinking, as Lolita had never worked a day in her life, except at being Lolita. I'm husbanded out, she thought. I wouldn't mind strolling into some boutique around ten and strolling out around three, after a nice long lunch that's paid for by the shop. I would love to pop down off a stool whenever a customer came in. I'm good at that. She also thought it would be fun to set the timers at a tanning salon. Hell, she'd already learned to set her own at Christophe's; why not get paid for it? Yet standing in the kitchen, tugged by opposing ... *forces* would be too strong a word; *nouns* is perhaps better – lethargy and boredom –

she just couldn't muster enough energy to pick up the phone and make some inquiries in the job market. However, a few seconds later, when her cordless coincidentally rang, the sensory jolt provided her with enough current to get her arms moving, and she answered the phone.

'Don't you hula hoop?' It was her friend Christine from the beauty salon, calling to say that one of her clients was looking for someone to teach hula hoop to a child star for a movie that was set in the sixties. 'To get the job, you have to meet a guy named Laszlo for an interview. Here's his number.' It was the perfect moment, and the suggestion electrocharged the dormant section of her brain called 'work.' In the time it took the phone to travel from her ear to its cradle, Lolita had decided to put on her other yellow mini and drive into Burbank for an appointment with Laszlo.

Laszlo, who looked more like a Morty, sat in what was a surprisingly dingy office for someone who must be such a big movie executive. Lolita responded to his first no-eye-contact question: 'Name?'

'Lo-lee-tah.' She spoke her name like a steam radiator with consonants.

'Last name?'

'Lolita Rooney-Burton-Winn-Fortensky-Guccioni,'

she said, omitting a few names for time and adding a few to jazz it up.

'Education?'

Uncomfortable, Lolita squeaked in her seat as the polyester of her dress skidded in the shellacked chair. 'Couldn't we do this on the golf course?' she asked. Laszlo squinched his face into a question mark, glanced up at Lolita for the first time, looked over at his wall clock, then snapped his chin once, signifying, Let's go.

Lolita's body was particularly suited for golf, whereas her interlocutor's wasn't. Laszlo swung his three wood as though he were using it to drive a nail into a garden. Sometimes Laszlo's ball would accidentally squirt forward; sometimes it would be driven into the dirt, where it looked like a buried eyeball. Lolita's swing, on the other hand, was a beautiful thing even to *hear*: a long accelerating *whoosh*, broken by a bullwhip crack in its fat center. There was also the three-act stage play of Lolita setting the ball down on the tee. Only this time it wasn't box boys and checkout girls watching; it was money managers and stock traders – all embryo husbands, waiting to be born. In her yellow mini, she looked like a small sun rolling from green to green. By the end of the game, not only had

Lolita won the job; she had also sold her house to the pro.

When the money came in, three months later, Lolita bought a two-story California-style in West Hollywood and nestled herself between the clink of Beverly Hills gold plate on one side and a self-reliant gay enclave on the other. The only negative consequence of the move was that her supermarket forays no longer had the desired effect. Box boys, instead of giving her the once-over, would now simply spot-check her for an Adam's apple.

Lolita's new location, only seventeen miles from her old one, was a total reformation in lifestyle. She had a string of dates, some of them with the deeply smitten Laszlo, and she conducted her hula hoop class on an almost regular basis, which brought in extra money for facials and massages. Her fourth husband, Leo, the one she really loved, would pop over occasionally, bringing a gift basket from a Beverly Hills bath shop, and sometimes she would smooch with him in return, but that was all. She was invited to premieres and gallery openings, and she could walk into Beverly Hills to the Pay-Less for the autobronzing cream she now favored over the tanning salons. Lolita's life had metamorphosed, as it always did, with an easy glide and a minimum of effort.

Now, sublimely niched into her new life, with all her powers working utterly, having applied a light touch of makeup in case of an early postal delivery, she slides into the puff pastry that is her bed and glances over at the newly antique photo of a middle-aged man named Humbert, which she has resurrected from the back of a dresser drawer during the move. She looks around the bedroom, which is high enough and secure enough to let her sleep with the window open, and bathes herself in two fine thoughts: that all her lovers have been true, and that her life keeps getting better and better.

The Hundred Greatest Books That I've Read

1. *The A-Bomb and Your School Desk*
2. *Little Lulu*, number 24, January, 1954
3. The *Weekly Reader* humor column
4. Women Love It If You're Funny! (advertisement)
5. *Robert Orben's Patter for Magicians*
6. The book that starts, 'It was the best of times; it was the worst of times.'
7. *Silas Marner* (first and last page only)
8. *Catcher in the Rye*, J. D. Salinger
9. *Sex for Teenagers*, pamphlet, 1962
10. *The Nude* (serious art photos)
11. *Lolita* (movie only)
12. *New Owners Manual, 1966 Mustang*
13. *Showmanship for Magicians*, by Daryl Fitzkee
14. *The Republic*, by Plato
15. *Steal this Book*, by Abbie Hoffman
16. *Fasting with the Proper Incense*, by 'Free'
17. *Being and Nothingness*, Jean-Paul Sartre

18. *Being and Nothingness*, Cliffs Notes
19. *The Complete Works of Shelley*
21. *How For Two Years to Never Once Speak to the Girl of Your Dreams, Even Though You Sit Across from Her Everyday in the College Library*, by Iggy Carbanza
22. *How to Seduce Women by Being Withdrawn, Falsely Poetic, Quiet and Moody*, (same author)
23. *The Expert at the Card Table*, S. R. Erdnase
24. *Hamlet* (screenplay)
25. *The Banjo and Marijuana: Delusions of Grandeur*, by Snuffy Grubbs
26. *A Coney Island of the Mind*, by Lawrence Ferlinghetti
27. *Why It's Not Important to Have a Fancy Table at a Restaurant*, by D. Jones
28. *Journey to Ixtlan*, by Carlos Casteneda
29. *Who to Call When You're Busted for Peyote*, by officer P. R. Gainsly
30. *What to Read on Your Summer Vacation*, published by the New York Public Library
31. *Tess of the D'Urbevilles*, by Thomas Hardy
32. *The Idiot*, by Dostoyevsky
33. *The Playboy Advisor* (letters about stereo equipment only)

34. *What Night Club Audiences are Like in Utah*, by 'Tippy' Tibbs

35. *Fifty Great Spots for Self-Immolation in Bryce Canyon*, by 'Tippy' Tibbs (now deceased)

36. *Great Laundromats of the Southwest*, by the General Services Administration

37. *Using Hypnotism to Eliminate the Word 'Like' from Your Vocabulary*, by Swami Helatious

38. 'The Hollywood Hot 100' (article)

39. *How to Not Let Anyone Know You're Having a Panic Attack*, by E. K. G.

40. 'The Hollywood Hot 100' (rechecking)

41. 'Whatever Happened to . . . ?' (article)

42. *If You're Not Happy When Everything Good is Happening to You, You Must be Insane*, by Loopy d'Lulu

43. *The Nouveau Riche, and its Attraction to Silver Bathroom Wallpaper*, by Paige Rense

44. *How to Bid at Sotheby's*, (six volumes)

45. *Thinking You're a Genius in the Art Market Until 1989*, by Warren Buffet

46. *Beating the Experts at Chinese Ceramics*, by Taiwan Tony

47. *Selling Your Fake Chinese Ceramics*, by Taiwan Tony

48. *Windows for Dummies*

49. *Windows for Idiots*
50. *Windows for the Sub-human*
51. *Fifty Annoying Sinus Infections You Can Legally Give Bill Gates*, by Steve Jobs
52. *Romeo and Juliet* by William Shakespeare
53. *Great Love Poems*, collection
54. *Martha Stewart's Wedding Book*
55. *Men are from Mars, Women are from Venus*, by John Gray (gift)
56. *How Come You Don' Listen to Me No Mo'?*, by Dr Grady Ulose (gift)
57. *Ten Lousy Things Men Do to be Rotten*, by Dr Laura Sleshslinger (gift)
58. *Crummy Men Who Can't Think and Don' Do Nothin'* by Jersey Delius (gift)
59. *Pre-nup Loopholes, by Anon., Esq.*
60. *How to Survive the Loss of a Love*, Prelude Press
61. *How to Get Over a Broken Love Affair*
62. *Mourning is Your Best Friend*
63. *Be a Man, Get Over It!*
64. *Diagnostic Manual of Mental Disorders*, American Psychiatric Association
65. *Get Ready to Live!* By H. Camper
66. *Omelet:Olga, Mnemonic Devices for Remembering Waitresses' Names*

67. *Victoria's Secret*, fall catalogue
68. *Your Stomach, and Why It's So Fat*
69. *Inappropriate Dating and Your Hair*, by
    Spraon Brown
70. *Male Menopause*, by Jed Diamond
71. *He*, by Robert Johnson
72. *Him, a Journey into the Male Psyche*, by Abel
    Macintosh
73. *The Male Within*, Dr Ken Justin
74. *It's a Guy Thing*, by 'Jesse' (convicted felon)
75. *What Breasts Can Make You Do*, by Joseph
    Keen
76. *Owners Manual for the Harley Davidson
    'Sportster' 883*
77. *One Hundred Worst Movies of the 80s*
78. *Bonding with the Feminine*
79. *Bringing out the Feminine*
80. *Loving your Anima*
81. *Life Begins at Forty, Too Bad You're Fifty*, by
    Trini Montana
82. *It's Time to Leave Childish Humor Behind*, by
    Ayed Lykta Dooya
83. *How Methadone Can Help Cure Your
    Chap-Stick Addiction*, doctor's office
    pamphlet
84. *Ulysses*, by James Joyce (first sentence only)

Closure

Closure. I wanted it. Or I wasn't going to be able to move on. The taxi had dropped me off fully ten blocks earlier than I had requested. Sixty-first instead of seventy-first. Luckily, I had copied down the cab number in case for some reason I needed closure. This time I did. I called the taxi company from my cell phone. I told them what I wanted. 'Some kind of closure,' I said. 'I need to get on with my life.' They understood. Thus the day had begun.

It was a little matter of a short-change at the supermarket. One dollar and fifty cents. Not much, but as I stood there counting the change, realizing the mistake, I couldn't move on. I confronted the check-out girl. 'Oops,' she said. Oops? Oops? This was not closure. How was I to move on? I did not sense that the store was taking responsibility. The manager came over and took me aside. He understood closure. He apologized, and took responsibility. I was lucky. I could move on.

My girlfriend Josie was already at the apartment. I had given her a key just two weeks earlier. I came in with the groceries. We put them away and ordered in. We watched the news. Murder, larceny, confidence games: so many people who couldn't move on. I kissed her and held her hand. I took her to the bedroom. I tried to make love to her, but couldn't. Too many loose ends. But she wanted closure. I explained that because so many people in my life weren't taking responsibility, it became impossible for me to accept my own responsibility. She understood. But she still wanted closure.

Two days go by. My movie theatre free admission coupon is not being honored. A line forms behind me as I explain my situation to the ticket seller. I had called ahead to make sure it would be honored. They said it would be. Yet here I am, being embarrassed in front of strangers. Josie says 'Let's pay,' and suggests that we move on. I cannot. I tell them I will need closure. The man selling tickets says the coupon people made a mistake and they are the ones who will need to take responsibility. 'So you need closure,' I say. 'Yes,' he replies, 'before we can move on.' 'So my closure is dependent on your closure,' I say. 'Yes.' Just then Josie says, 'I need closure too, tonight.' She pays. I move on, even though I am unable to move on.

We watch the movie. It is about Mary Queen of Scots. She was beheaded. At least she got closure. When the movie is over, it says, 'The end.' We can go home.

Pop goes the champagne cork. Josie starts drinking. I start to worry. She starts kissing me. I am helpless. I can't move on. The phone rings and the machine picks up. It's the manager of the movie theatre. 'I talked with the coupon people,' he says, 'they will issue a new coupon. I'm hoping now we can move on.' I smile at Josie. But something's still not right. I notice the answering machine blinking. I irritate Josie when I play back the message. It is the taxi company with a full apology. I can move on.

I give Josie closure. She snuggles next to me. A candle burns to the end and snuffs itself out. The moonlight trickles into the bedroom. I look at the bedroom door. It's ajar. I know what I need.

The Y3K Bug

With only eight years to go before the end of the third millennium, many scientists are beginning to express their concern with the Tridecta Blighter Function whose circuitry was not programmed to accommodate the year 3000. 'Who knew people would live six hundred years?' said Tyrell Oven-Baby Number 9, whose work in Danish metao-scillititaniannia led the way to the Fundolator. 'Yes,' continued Number 9, 'at the stroke of midnight, some people's heads will explode. Naturally, they will grow back, but the problem is, they will keep exploding for the rest of their lives. This will be fine for the New Year's celebration, but I think most people would want it to stop by Dirndl Day.'

Of course, all of us have had our heads regenerated at one time or another, so why the fuss? The problem is that most of us with a Tridecta Blighter Function that was implanted in our duodenum before the year

2465, will lose the use of two of our penises. This will leave most of us with our eight vaginas but only six functioning male organs. Yes, it is possible to get along with only six penises, but what about our quality of life?

Some experts have stated that the problem is overrated, that *at worst* a head may explode seven or eight times, and since most people today keep their heads at home in an aluminum box, what difference will it make? Some people counter by claiming that this is a *moral* issue. We have a right for our heads to explode when *we* want them to, and not because a corporate giant failed to look six hundred years into the future. This is as fundamental a right, they claim, as the right to redirect the world's rivers for personal gain, as the right to re-hem anyone's outer garments, or the right to govern one of the lesser races, such as the Offspring of Jerry Springer's Guests, who live in Tarzana.

Many people worry that the Y3K bug will interfere with the holidays. Perhaps the old Gregorian calendar might have been affected, whose major holidays were Christmas and Easter, but not the Jordanian calendar, introduced by Michael Jordan in the first decade of the twenty-first century. The Jordanian calendar, centered around the three major televised holidays – The Superbowl, the Oscars and the Basketball playoffs – only requires a six-second delay at the start of the third quarter of the basketball semi-finals every twenty-six years to keep it accurate. The three-day weekend of Easter, Christmas and Rosh Shashona should not be affected.

What Can I Do?

Try to Relax. When New Year's Eve rolls around, put on an old movie, such as the hilarious comedy *2001*. Or treat yourself to a glass of water. This also might be a good time to plug up any oozing plasma you might have. Be sure to use the newer molded living mouse plugs rather than the old polyhydrine ones. The living mouse plugs do a better job, and many people like having a pet poking out of their bodies.

Take a Trip! Forget your troubles, and go see a real twentieth-century house. Be prepared to see a residence where the ceilings are eight feet high! Nowadays, when people are bumping their heads on twenty-foot ceilings, the sight of these Lilliputian homes always brings a tickle to the funny bone, which is safely kept in your funny-bone jar at home.

Stay Home and Let Your Head Blow Up. The worst thing that happens is that you're out of commission until you can grow a new one. We all know what a peaceful time that is, when no faxes ring in your head and no b-mail messages are delivered to your right hemisphere from President Pete.

What Happens if My Head Blows Up and I'm at a Party?

Everyone will know about the Y3K bug, and most likely you won't be the only one to explode. There will also be a tendency for everyone to step back from everyone else when the clock strikes midnight. However, you will have to be prepared for those unkind people who will taunt you by calling you 'ol' six penis.'

In spite of all these tips, there are those of you who still might not be easy about the coming new millennium and it's accompanying problems. If you can't quite relax, remember these words spoken last week by the chairman of the Inner Planets:

Everything's going to be okay. Be sure to watch our two-hour special, brought to you by Andromeda, where we recap the music of the millennium.

DICK CLARK

A Word from the Words

First, let me say how much I enjoy being one of the words in this book and how grateful I am for this opportunity to speak for the whole group. Often we're so busy speaking for others that we never get to speak for ourselves, or directly to you, the reader. I guess it's redundant to say 'you, the reader,' but we're not used to writing, and it sounds better to my ear than, say, 'you, the two giant fists that are holding me' or 'you, the large, heavy mass of protoplasm.'

There's also a nice variety of words in this book, and that always makes it fun. We can hang around with the tough utilitarian words, like *the*, and have a few beers, or we can wander over and visit the lofty *perambulate*, who turned out to be a very nice verb with a very lovely wife, *tutu*. *Fuzzy* also turned out to be a lot of fun; she had a great sense of humor and a welcoming manner that we all learned from. I can never decide whether I'd like to be proletariat or bourgeois in this world of words. The common words, such as the pronouns and the transitive verbs, get used a lot, but they're tired (you should see them running around here, carrying their objects). The exciting words, like *fo'c'sle*, make a lot of impact but aren't frequently called into service. I'm lucky. I'm *underpants*. Sometimes I'm used innocuously, but other times I get to be in very racy sentences in some pretty damn good books. Of course, some usages I find shocking. Which is a point I'd like to make: When you read something that disgusts you, don't blame the word. *Scrotum* goes around here like someone just shot his best friend, but really he's a legitimate guy who gets used in ugly ways by a lot of cheeseballs. Likewise *pimple*. I was there when he got used as 'a pimple on the face of humanity.' The poor guy was blue for a month. He walked around here with a hangdog look and even tried to be friends with *hangdog look*, but around here, a phrase won't mingle with a word; they just won't. It also irks me that two ordinary words can be given a hyphen and suddenly they're all-important. Me? Of course I would love to be a proper noun, but I'm not, so that's that. Even with the current fad of giving children unusual names, it's unlikely that any couple will call a newborn *Underpants*.

This is also my first experience being on a page, since my typing on January 23 (birthday coming up!). When I was a computer word, things were great. I could blast through cyberspace, scroll across screens, travel to India. Now that I'm on the page, I'm worried that it's going to be mostly dark. My request to you, the person above me, with the two gigantic lenses over your eyes, is that you occasionally open the book after you have finished reading it and give all of us a little air. A simple thumbing through will do. Not that I'm unhappy in here. There are enough diverse words that our little civilization can keep itself amused for the twenty or so years we expect to be on a shelf, or stacked in a corner, or sold in a garage.

I'd also like to say something to you budding writers. Believe me, I do understand that sometimes it's essential to use incorrect grammar. That is fine with me, and the words who are in those sentences are aware of their lot in life. But it's difficult to even hang around an incomplete sentence, much less be in one. I imagine it's like talking to a person whose head is missing. It just doesn't feel right. A friend of mine has been misspelled in a computer file for over fourteen years, and it doesn't look like he's ever going to be spell-checked.

There are a couple of individuals who would like to speak:

I'm the word *sidle*, and it was fun to be in that story about the dog (I couldn't see the title from where I was).

Greetings. I'm *scummy*, and I'd like to mention that you are a lowlife.

Hello. I'm *hello*, and I'd like to say myself.

And now we'd like to hear from a group of individuals without whom none of the work we do would be possible:

Hi. We're the letters, and we'd just like to say that we enjoy being a part of the very fine words on this page. Thank you.

And last but not least, someone very special to the whole crew here in *Pure Drivel* would like to end this book:

?

Permissions

The publishers wish to thank the copyright holders of the following song lyrics for permission to reprint them in this volume:

'I Feel Pretty' from *West Side Story* by Leonard Bernstein © copyright 1956, 1957, 1958, 1959 by The Estate of Leonard Bernstein and Stephen Sondheim. Copyright renewed. Leonard Bernstein Music Publishing Company Plc, Publisher. Boosey & Hawkes, Inc., Sole agent. International copyright secured.

'Heat Wave', words and music by Irving Berlin © 1933 Irving Berlin Music Corp. Warner/Chappell Music Ltd, London W6 8BS. Reproduced by permission of IMP Ltd.

The following pieces were originally published in *The New Yorker* magazine: 'A Public Apology';

'Writing Is Easy'; 'Yes, in My Own Backyard'; 'Changes in the Memory after Fifty'; 'Dear Amanda'; 'Times Roman Font Announces Shortage of Periods'; 'Taping My Friends'; 'The Paparazzi of Plato'; 'Side Effects'; 'How I Joined Mensa'; 'Drivel'; 'In Search of the Wily Filipino'.

The following was originally published in *The New York Times Magazine*: 'The Nature of Matter and Its Antecedents'.

The following was originally published in *The New York Times* op-ed section: 'Mars Probe Finds Kittens'.